FULL CIRCLE

FULL CIRCLE

A Quest for Transformation

JUAN-LORENZO HINOJOSA
RAVEN HINOJOSA

FULL CIRCLE
A Quest for Transformation

Juan-Lorenzo Hinojosa
Raven Hinojosa

Edited by Gregory F. Augustine Pierce
Cover design by Christin Hinojosa-Kirschenbaum
Text design and typesetting by Patricia A. Lynch
Cover background by David M. Schrader, Adobe Stock
Cover image by Croisy, Adobe Stock

Copyright © 2021 by Juan-Lorenzo Hinojosa and Raven Hinojosa

Published by ACTA Publications, 4848 N. Clark Street,
Chicago, IL 60640, (800) 397-2282, www.actapublications.com

All rights reserved. No part of this publication may be reproduced or transmitted in any form or by any means, electronic or mechanical, including photocopying and recording, or by any information storage and retrieval system, including the Internet, without permission from the publisher. Permission is hereby given to use short excerpts or pieces of art with proper citation in reviews and marketing copy, church bulletins and handouts, and scholarly papers.

Library of Congress Catalog number: 2021935251
ISBN: 978-0-87946-694-7
Printed in the United States of America by Total Printing Systems
Year 35 34 33 32 31 30 29 28 27 26 25 24 23 22 21
Printing 15 14 13 12 11 10 9 8 7 6 5 4 3 2 First

♲ Text printed on 30% post-consumer recycled paper

TABLE OF CONTENTS

•••

•••

•••

•••

...

To Sarah, my wife and the love of my life,
who helped with
the initial editing of this book
and with everything I have written over the years.
And to my dear children, especially Raven,
who co-wrote this book with me.

...

Testimony of a Twice Born

BY JUAN-LORENZO

...

William James, the great psychologist and philosopher of religion who wrote his classic book, *The Varieties of Religious Experience* in 1902, describes two fundamental types of religious experience — that of the "once born" and that of the "twice born." The story you are about to read is that of someone who has been twice born. The spiritual vignette I share immediately in the first chapter is the inflection point of my twice-born journey.

This book is written as a testimony. A testimony is given by a witness who has experienced something. This is my witness. I have told and retold the most central elements of this story verbally. I first told it when I was in my early twenties, immediately after I returned from the U.S. to Bolivia in 1968 to spend time with my father and stepmother. They insisted I see a psychiatrist, and the psychiatrist diagnosed psychosis in what I am about to share with you. I decided to go see a wise Jesuit priest I knew, and that Jesuit saw a valuable spiritual experience. I dropped the psychiatrist and went with the priest!

Here is the gist of the story. I was baptized a Catholic, but I did not accept the tradition as my own until I had a personal mystical experience of God. To be clear, God is certainly not an old white man in the sky. God cannot even be called a "supreme being," because the reality is far beyond that category...or any other. In our time, to even use the word "God" underlines those limiting notions. That is why I use the term "Holy Mystery" instead. I feel that this is a way to reference, in one term, the limits of human concepts, our own reverence, and the real-ness of the holy.

At its core, this is a story about vocation. Frederick Buechner has aptly described vocation as "the place where one's deep gladness meets the world's deep hunger." We humans discover our vocation by discerning our deep longings and gifts and then aligning our lives with Holy Mystery's project in history. But even after having my sense of my own vocation firmly in hand, my family and work life have not proceeded without struggle, wrong turns, and false starts. Contrary to popular understanding, having a vocation does not demand a settled path or even a clear goal. Stumbling is integral to life. For example, when a car is stationary it is very difficult to turn the steering wheel. When it's moving, the wheel turns easily. It is only in moving forward that we can adjust our vocational direction.

I believe that hearing and answering a vocational calling is deeply connected to being on a spiritual path. This is the story of how I found that path and learned to hear that call for myself. Holy Mystery speaks to us in our everyday world. We can experience our call in the form of intuition, synchronicity, circumstances, and felt knowledge. These often are connected to and shaped by our individual religious/spiritual traditions. If we are responsive to the guidance we receive and engage the actual realities of our lives in our response, we will live our lives well and fulfill the potential of our lives.

Spiritual reality exists whether we acknowledge it or not, and it springs from its own loving, self-giving nature. We are called to surrender to this spiritual reality and moral order and then to live within it. Spiritual faith and faithfulness provide us with a new horizon that changes everything.

•••

This book is co-written by my daughter Raven and myself. She is the only one of our five children to use a name not given at birth. I share that distinction with her, as "Lorenzo" is a name given to me when I was twenty-one. Her writing gifts were needed. She also has something we share. We have taken different spiritual paths, but we deeply share an appreciation for the spiritual dimension of reality. It has been a joy and blessing to work with her on the story you are about to read.

The structure of the book is somewhat unusual. It has four first-person expositions written by me and 12 third-person biographical vignettes about my life, originally told by me but recounted here by Raven — the two complementing each other to tell the story of my quest for transformation in my life. Several intense spiritual experiences I had over the course of one momentous year are recounted in four first-person expositions, starting with the first one right after this Introduction and continuing in three others interspersed within the biographical vignettes. Raven's sensibility and skill as the writer have made my story a more compelling narrative. My limited communication talents lie in other directions, but the writing in the expositions about my spiritual experiences is my own, albeit with help from Raven. I have also included two appendices at the end of the book. The first consists of short theological essays I have written reflecting on my life as a whole, including some of the events recounted by Raven. The second is a timeline of my life for those who might be confused by the back and forth in time and continents that takes place in the book.

My memoir has two parts, as any "twice born" person tends to have: a before and an after.

I begin with my "Mirror Experience," and after "The Inflection Point" go on to the rest of my life. You will find that there are various names attached to me in my story. As an infant, I was baptized Juan Carlos Tadeo Hinojosa de Avila. As a child, because Charles is English for Carlos, I had the nickname Charly. When I was sent to military school, I was called Johnny, because John is English for Juan. In the "after" time, my name became what it is today, Juan-Lorenzo, with a hyphen.

I have come to believe, with St. Paul, that in God "we live, move, and have our being." This story is my experience of that truth.

The Mirror Experience

BY JUAN-LORENZO

• • •

It was 1968 and I had been living in Haight Ashbury in San Francisco since 1966. I began to let certain elements of my life in the Haight fall away. I stopped going out with women. I stopped smoking marijuana or dropping acid or taking mezcaline. My curiosity was satisfied, and I simply felt that a change was upon me. I began a strict macrobiotic diet, and my already lean body started dropping pounds.

It was mid-afternoon in December when I let myself in and threw my keys on the table. My apartment was one of the few in the building that made use of the lock on the door. The rest of the flats on Stanyan Street were occupied by hippies who were either too high to manage keys or kept their doors open on the principle of the "free" society. I had always been more private. I also had plenty of acid (LSD) sitting in a kitchen drawer and fat rolls of money in a shoe box under the sink from a year of dealing. It was a good deal of money.

That afternoon, I ran my fingers through the coarse hair of my beard, shrugged off my corduroy jacket, and hung it neatly in the closet. Some habits from military school are hard to shake. It was one of those bright San Francisco days where the air is sharp and cool, but the sun feels hot when you stop to soak it in. I stepped onto the patio and into a slant of sunshine. Bright, hot; I pulled off my sweater to let the rays warm my arms. Then, as if from nowhere, it happened.

Afterwards, I would think of the experience as a gift from Holy Mystery and use words like "infused knowledge" to try to explain it. But at that time I wouldn't have thought in those terms and, anyway, these are inadequate words for an experience unbreachable by language, even in metaphor.

I was facing the overgrown outside wall of my building, relaxing into the sunlight. I was thinking about nothing in particular, when suddenly and unquestionably, reality shifted all around me. My body felt light. My feet, which were planted on the crumbling brick patio, felt unmoored, as though I might float away at any moment. A rush of energy entered the space around me, my body included, and just like that — I knew. Unlike the psychedelic trips I'd taken earlier in the year, where layers of reality seemed to be revealed, in this strange state the only thing exposed was myself. My character, true motivations, and the consequences of my actions became unbearably clear — as clear as if I were looking into a mirror that showed only the truths I denied.

I realized that my belief in the hippie paradigm had been subverted into a shallowly-held justification to do anything I pleased. My life was being spent in the pursuit of vacant pleasures. My heart broke open and I felt in one terrible flood every bit of the anxiety and betrayal I had caused my parents, my girlfriends, and — under the glib business of debauchery — myself. In that moment of vicious clarity, I saw right past Johnny to Juan Carlos Tadeo Hinojosa de Avila.

Then, suddenly, I saw beyond even that person to the person I had the potential to become. It was a revelatory insight that surpassed my own capacity for perception or judgment. I didn't think it; I just knew it. It revealed every part of myself I had most tried to avoid knowing, right down to the content of my own soul. It was a moment of great personal pain, but it was also instantly freeing. It moved me in a way that meant that everything had to change. It moved me so deeply that, as the moment faded away and my mundane consciousness returned, I knew that everything already had changed for good and forever. I had been shown the possibility of a new way forward and now was meant to find it.

Charly in Bolivia

BY RAVEN

•••

It was 1954, two years after Charly and his family returned to Bolivia from the United States, and everything was different. At eight years old, Charly felt he'd already seen a lot of the world. His mother told him his first trip had been at two months old, when they'd moved to Pennsylvania for *Papá's* schooling. He didn't remember that, but he did remember moving back again.

It had been his sixth birthday, and *Mamá*, his brother Junior, and the captain of the steamer ship had cake with him as they crossed the Panama Canal and the shores of South America came into view. He had wished for a red Radio Flyer wagon for his birthday, like the one he had left behind. As it turned out, even Sears and Roebuck couldn't ship a Radio Flyer to Bolivia.

Charly turned over in bed, remembered it was Saturday, and popped up. A day with no school was a good day for him. In the U.S., he had been at the head of his first-grade class, but in Bolivia he was "still adjusting," as Mamá said. It wasn't the language, because he had always spoken Spanish at home. It was the funny way they did things in Bolivia. For example, Charly had been a master of the ballpoint pen back in Philadelphia, and now he had to write with something called a "nib" that you dipped into an inkwell sunk into an ancient-looking desk. The teacher didn't ask questions, and you weren't allowed to ask her any. Unless you were called on to recite whatever you were memorizing that week, you had to remain silent. Papá called it "backwards." Charly called it crazy.

He padded downstairs to the kitchen in back of the house, where he found Ernesta and Paola, the housemaid and cook. Mamá usually sat with him at breakfast, but he could already see this was a day she would be too busy. Caterers were moving around the huge house, setting up something out on the lawn and placing an enormous bouquet in the foyer. In the United States, they had lived in apartments or very small houses and had moved often. The only parties he remembered had been birthday parties at the kitchen table for himself and his brother. Ever since they'd moved back to the city of La Paz and into this big house in the south of the city, his parents often had parties of a much different scale.

In the kitchen, Paola and Ernesta chatted about the guests coming that night. Charly didn't understand their indigenous language, Quechua, but they said some things in Spanish, like "the Petroleum Minister of Peru" and "the American Ambassador." After finishing his tea and bread slathered with *dulce de leche* and not finding

6

Junior around, he decided to get dressed and go into the city by himself. Papá often worked on a Saturday, and when he did, Charly was allowed to ride the bus uptown to his office for a visit. He found his mother, who hugged him, fussed with his hair, and gave him some coins for the bus fare. He was off.

Little Charly grinned when the bus pulled up and he saw it was one of his favorites. In Bolivia, many of the small buses were artfully and colorfully painted, and he remembered this one by its golden sun. Once aboard, he slipped into a seat between a window and a *cholita* with enormous skirts and a chicken on her lap. Despite the crowd, her black eyes wore a placid expression above her smooth, wind-burned cheeks. She looked kind, but she didn't talk to him. The *indios* very seldom did. The route uphill to the office was a straight shot up the Avenida Arce. Through the dust-caked window, Charly's gaze was drawn upward. La Paz is a city in a deep valley, built in a bowl made by the Andes mountains. Behind them, majestic Mount Illimani towered in the distance, with its snow-covered triple peaks. Little houses in pastel colors crawled up the sides of the bowl on three sides, until the land suddenly plateaued onto the barren, flat Altiplano, where the slums were beginning to grow like weeds as many indigenous people moved in from the countryside.

• • •

When the bus jolted through a certain intersection, Charly remembered taking a recent trip up that very street with his father. Papá had brought him along on a visit to the city's public hospital. They didn't ride a bus that day. They drove in a limo with his father's company chauffeur, uphill and through the front gates of a big colonial building in crumbling disrepair. Inside, they were led into a room occupied by men who had been burned in an oil-well explosion. Remembering the smell that hit him coming through the door, even now Charly felt his stomach turn. The men they visited had been injured badly and were covered in bandages, some even over their faces. One was naked and sitting in a bathtub full of ice cubes, and before the nurse pulled the curtain closed Charly could see the man's blood-red flesh. Papá sat and talked to the men and gently put his hand on top of their bandaged hands. Charly thought his Papá was very good to do this, but the things he remembered most were the rickety cots and all the shabby things in the room. Everything seemed so poor and so broken down. The wheelchairs were not the modern kind made of metal, like the one he'd seen his Aunt Blanca use when she broke her ankle. These were made of wood and had wicker seats with holes in them. He hoped the men wouldn't have to ride in them once they were well enough to leave the room, which he assumed they would be soon.

•••

Jolted from his revery, Charly realized the Mercado Camacho was coming up on the left. This was his stop. He squeezed past women in embroidered shawls and over the feet of men in sandals made from tire tread, landing on the sidewalk in front of the building for the Bolivian national oil company, or YPFB. The doorman and all the receptionists knew him and said hello, and soon he was on the floor that was his Papá's office. It was full of chrome and brightly colored leather seating, with lots of men in suits and pretty women who smelled of perfume and pinched his cheeks. Everyone was in a hurry there all the time, but it was quiet on this Saturday.

Charly went to sit with Señora Gonzalez behind the big desk outside Papá's door and eat cookies while the secretary answered phone calls. He could see through the glass door into the office. His father was signing papers and giving them one by one to a man in a blue suit. Finally, he looked up and gave his son a wave and three fingers. Charly knew this meant he would be busy for at least half an hour, and he decided to go to the Mercado Camacho instead of waiting.

Downstairs and across the street, the sprawling market could not have been more different from the atmosphere of the office. It was open to the air, which in 12,500-foot-high La Paz was achingly dry, cold in the shade, and hot in the sun. Rows of vendors in stalls sold hot food and dry goods. Charly liked wandering near the back where there was a row selling only musical instruments and another with the things *cholitas* wore, like gathered skirts and bowler hats. His favorite rows were the lines of women sitting on the ground surrounded by their produce, fruit, and flowers. They seemed like mountain flowers themselves, the way they seemed to sprout out of the mounds of their skirts. He bought a packet of candy for his Mamá before making his way back to the office.

• • •

Late that night, Charly crouched outside his bedroom door and peered through the wrought iron of the interior balcony overlooking the party below. The men were all dressed identically in black tuxedos, and the women wore gloves and jewelry that shimmered against their necks. He saw his older brother, Junior, now a gangly teenager, disappear into the kitchen with a girlfriend. That man standing with his Papá must be the American Ambassador he'd

9

heard mentioned earlier. And Charly already knew the man standing with them was the President of Bolivia, Victor Paz Estenssoro. Charly thought about what the gardener had told him, that the president was a good man because he gave the Indians the right to vote and to be educated. These were big changes, and everyone seemed to have an opinion.

"*Ya era hora,*" said, "It was about time."

But that morning at Papá's office, he'd heard Señora Gonzalez say the opposite. "The revolution isn't good for anybody, not even those Indians."

Charly scanned the crowd one last time for his mother and didn't find her. She'd had another terrible headache today. There had been a fight with Papá too. Finally, he thought to find her in her room. It was very dark, and she was lying down in her gown, with all her jewelry on.

He stood beside the bed and spoke softly. "Why are you crying, Mamá?"

"It's only my headache, *mi hijito,*" she whispered, and held out her arms for him to crawl in beside her. He fell asleep listening to the sounds of laughter and piano music from down below.

Johnny Back in the U.S.

BY RAVEN

Charly lay awake, staring at the slats of the bunk above him. So much had happened since he had come back to the U.S. that he felt he must be a different person by now. It had started back in Bolivia, with his parents' divorce. One day the family was living life as usual in their big house in La Paz, and the next he and his mother were living with relatives in Tartagal, Argentina. He'd finally realized his family was really and permanently changed when Christmas came and went and his father still wasn't there. Papá had a new family now, with a new wife who'd come with two sons of her own. Junior had been sent to a boarding school in the United States. After a year in Argentina, Charly and his mother had moved back to Philadelphia to live near Marta, Charly's half-sister from Mamá's first marriage. She was almost twenty years older than Charly, and he thought of Marta like a *tia*, an aunt. The money his father sent them might have supported them in Bolivia, but in the U.S. it didn't go far. They lived in a rough part of town. As a Latino, a "spic," he didn't fit in with the Euro-American kids at school or the African-American kids in the neighborhood. He had been in some fights, his mother had become concerned, and now he was in military school.

"So, that's the one thing Eduardo will pay for?" he had heard Marta say to Mamá about Papá the night before Charly left for the academy, her voice shaking with indignation.

The divorce had happened ages ago, when he was only eight. Now he was thirteen. He wasn't even called Charly anymore, his baby name, or Juan Carlos, as he had been called in school in Bolivia. In the U.S., he had become Johnny. Thinking of his baby name made him think of his mother, who was never far from his mind. Two months ago, he had been told by one of the school's administrators to pack a bag because he was going to visit his mother in the hospital.

"Is she sick?" he'd asked. They only answered that she was going in for an operation.

At the hospital, he stood next to her bed, and she told him she loved him with tears in her eyes. Johnny was confused. "But it's not dangerous, right?" He looked back at Marta and over at Junior.

Marta chimed in, "No, no, it isn't dangerous. It will all be over in a few hours. Go to my house and get some sleep."

•••

Late in the night, he was woken from a fitful sleep by Marta's husband, who put his hand on Johnny's shoulder and told him his mother had died on the operating table. Mamá was dead, and he didn't even get to say goodbye. Johnny immediately went into a state of shock and passed through the next few days like he was stumbling through a bad dream. He stayed with Marta. He went to his mother's funeral. He learned that she'd had a brain tumor and had suffered from it repeatedly for a number of years — but that seemed to Johnny like a stiff, incomprehensible piece of information, delivered much too late to be of any use. His mother, unlike his father, had always been there for him. She'd been the emotional center of his life. Now she was just…gone.

• • •

Several weeks later, Johnny shifted uncomfortably on his bottom bunk at military school, counting the minutes to the appointed time for his escape. He never would have considered something so drastic as running away from school when his mother was alive. He would have wanted to protect her feelings. There was no need for that now. He rolled from his left side to his right. It wasn't the bed that was so uncomfortable; it was the bruising on his bottom from the paddling he'd received at twenty-two hundred hours, just after lights out. His bruises hurt, but it was his pride that stung worst of all.

Johnny thought back to the first time he saw the very same paddle, almost two years ago, during his first week at Carson Long Military Academy. It had been the middle of the day when the adult lieutenant ordered everyone to stand at attention at the foot of their bunks in the large dorm room. The boys knew enough of the regimented schedule by then to know this was out of the ordinary. You could almost smell the fear in the big dorm room the sixth graders occupied. A boy was called to the front, someone

Johnny knew had a difficult time with discipline and authority. He was ordered to lower his pants and was paddled, hard. The lieutenant kept one eye on the reactions of the rest of the boys as he delivered swat after swat, sweating from exertion while calmly striking the boy. Though he stared straight ahead, Johnny could hear the air whistling through the holes cut in the vicious wooden paddle. He could hear the impact and the boy's whimpers.

That day, he'd realized that whatever the game was, it involved staying out of the way of that paddle. He made up his mind then that he would win that game. He would learn to deal with the expectations of the system in which he found himself. And he'd done just that. He was smaller than almost any other boy, but he was quick at the drills, intelligent, and a natural leader. He soon learned that the school had two distinct but interrelated power structures. One was official. There were merits, demerits, ranks, and positions. There was a strict hierarchy made up of students with rank, the upperclassmen, and the adult teachers and officers, all above Johnny by various degrees. He worked to be promoted to sergeant and then platoon leader, until he too was ranked above most of the boys in his class. He expected to be made an officer before the end of the year. The second power structure was less apparent, but to Johnny it was easier to understand than the seemingly arbitrary rules and decisions made by the adults. This one was between the boys themselves, who mimicked the overt system by creating their own internal pecking order through hazing, intimidation, and even sexual activity. Submission, which they called "respect," was demanded and enforced.

As far as Johnny was concerned, he had been punished that evening for merely playing by these rules, even if the adults didn't outwardly acknowledge them. He and his roommate Colin had decided to punish a kid who had a hard time staying neat and orderly. By dragging him out of bed and punching him in the hallway, they were only doing as they were expected to do. The poor kid did not deserve it, but they were playing by the "rules" as they knew them. Nevertheless, when the lights switched on while they were "disciplining" the kid, they could see by the purple face of the lieutenant that they were in for it. Along with the paddling, Johnny immediately lost his rank and position as platoon leader, the thing he had worked so relentlessly to earn. All that was over now.

Johnny glanced at the clock on the wall. It was time to go. He shouldered his small pack and crept into the dark hall along with Colin. Stealthily, they headed out into the night. Keeping to the shadows, they walked as far as the drill field and then began to run. They climbed the chain link fence on the far side and were finally in the woods. Johnny's heart was racing, and both boys let out intermittent muffled whoops and excited giggles as they crept along. The plan was to move as quickly as they could toward the highway, then follow it just behind the tree line until they could begin hitchhiking. They were headed to Colin's home some 200 miles away in Toms River, near the New Jersey coast. Colin kept looking behind them to see if they were being followed, but Johnny looked ahead. For the first time since arriving at the school, he felt free. For the first time since his mother's death, he felt something.

Their independence didn't last long. The two boys did manage to hitchhike from mid-Pennsylvania to New Jersey. When they arrived at Colin's home, however, they were met by Colin's parents, who immediately called the school. While the academy debated whether to expel them, the boys stayed at Colin's house and enjoyed having very little supervision. Colin introduced Johnny to girls, and they got drunk on beer — Charly's first time for both. After a few days, the school decided to take them back. It was clear from the first that they would be made an example of. All their privileges were revoked, and there was endless marching around the parade ground. Johnny remained rebellious in his attitude. The discipline only deepened his resentment.

Lucky for Johnny, the school year ended within a few weeks. His father reluctantly brought him back to South America, as the academy refused to admit him for another year. Papá had founded a new business and now lived in Buenos Aires with his second wife and their two daughters. Her sons by a previous marriage, as well as Johnny's big brother Junior, all lived at boarding schools. Johnny entered Eduardo's new household in Argentina with a significant chip on his shoulder and was greeted by his stepmother with a reluctance that bordered on disdain. In his own mind, his eyes had been opened, while everyone around him was sleepwalking. He wouldn't be fooled by the system again. His individuation had begun.

"Retiro" in Jail

BY RAVEN

Johnny paced and turned, paced and turned. The jail cell was seven paces up and seven paces down, with bunks for six men and a hole in the ground for their waste in one corner. For the hundredth time, he was reminded of the bunks back in military school. He felt lightheaded because he hadn't had a meal in two days. The main problem, as he went over it again and again in his mind, was that nobody knew where he was. He was a junior in high school at the American Community School in Buenos Aires. He was about to finish out the year and leave for the beach house in Punta del Este, Uruguay with his family, as he had each summer since moving back to South America three years ago. He knew his father and stepmother would be wondering about

17

him, and they would certainly be upset, but it had been the weekend. They probably assumed he had gone off with friends and not told them the details, just as he had on several other occasions. And if he didn't show up for school on Monday, that wasn't unusual either.

Johnny sat on his cot and glanced at the other men in the cell. Three were lying down, asleep or pretending to be. The one with the alcohol shakes was squatting over the toilet hole again. The one with the worn-out gaucho clothes, whose name was Diego, was leaning against the bars, looking back at him. No phone calls were allowed in Argentine jails, and the guards had ignored Johnny's requests to contact his father. One of these fellow prisoners would have to be released and be willing to get word to Johnny's family before anyone could even be aware where he was. And as long as no one knew he was in jail, he would get no food, as this was something that the prisoners' families were expected to provide from the outside.

Diego shifted positions, and Johnny looked up.

"*Retiro,*" Diego said.

The gaucho had given him a nickname, calling Johnny by the name of the upper-class neighborhood in Buenos Aires where he lived. In this way, he acknowledged in one word Johnny's affluent and urban origin.

"Yes, Diego?" said Johnny.

"You never told me what they pulled you in for. Skipping school?" Diego poked fun at him, but his laughter was not unkind.

"Stolen property," replied Johnny. "It was only a joy ride. I can't believe it. I would have left the car somewhere, and they would have found it in a couple of days, no harm done. I never had any trouble doing it before." As he explained himself, Johnny realized how spoiled he must sound, but he didn't know how to avoid it. He suddenly felt embarrassed and shook his head in frustration.

Diego smiled again. He had a wide smile with white teeth set against deep creases in his brown face. He could have been any age. He'd mentioned his young children though, so Johnny suspected that the laborer was younger than he looked. When he smiled, he squinted and his green eyes almost disappeared. Diego had already shared that he was imprisoned for debt, so Johnny didn't return the question. Instead, he felt a wave of lightheadedness and lay down on his bunk again, turning his face to the wall. He froze that way as he heard the guards open the metal doors. They yanked the man on the bunk across from him to his feet and out of the cell. He didn't know what the man had done, but he knew that the prison was known to use electric shock on inmates. Johnny was relieved he didn't have to watch him being taken away. When their footsteps faded down the hall, he turned over. Diego was no longer standing by the door but was sitting on his heels with a wooden bowl in front of him. It contained something that smelled wonderful. The guards must have brought it to him as they came for the other prisoner.

Johnny tried not to stare, but he found he couldn't turn his head away. Diego held the bowl out to him.

"From my wife," Diego said.

Johnny didn't resist. He joined Diego on the concrete floor and they both ate. It was gnocchi, an Italian potato pasta, and it was the most delicious thing Johnny had ever tasted. The next morning, Diego was released. He kept his word to call Johnny's father, even though he was poor and the phone call was not cheap. Papá came right away, and by the next day Johnny was back in high school. He would return to jail, in a total of four countries, in the

19

next few years, usually for drunkenness. He often remembered the generosity of the impoverished gaucho.

Johnny and Bobby in Buenos Aires

BY RAVEN

The following fall, Johnny and Bobby Aguirre perched at a bar in La Lucila on the outskirts of Buenos Aires. They ordered another round of Screwdrivers, slipping in and out of English and Spanish as they chatted and joked. Bobby was a stocky, shaggy-looking kid with large liquid brown eyes and a bit of a baby face. He was also a talker. He told stories and related gossip from the American School where the two young men were now both seniors but didn't actually attend regularly. Instead, they spent their time in Mi Boliche, their favorite bar. Though they were close friends, Bobby's chatter was nervous. Johnny mostly listened, but it was clear that he was leading the conversation and that Bobby adored him.

"And they just left him out there," said Bobby, throwing up

his hands.

Johnny shook his head. "Man, I never asked them to do that. I don't care about that stuff." He laughed in disbelief. "I don't think they really had a gun."

But Bobby insisted. "They had a gun! They drove way out of the city, man. Then they showed the gun and just left the guy."

Bobby was impressed with the gang from Mi Boliche, who were mostly young Argentine professionals. By going after this kid from the American School who'd made a move on Johnny's girl, they'd had his friend's back. They'd manhandled the kid into a car, scared him with a gun, and left him on a country road. Johnny thought the whole thing was a bit ridiculous.

Johnny and Bobby didn't quite fit in with the Euro-Americans at Lincoln and called themselves "half-breeds." The co-opted insult fit them both, as Johnny was a native Bolivian with a semi-American upbringing, and Bobby was half Mexican and half American. They thought of themselves as outsiders and wore the outsiders' styles of 1964. They acted tough, but Bobby was covering up a sensitive, intuitive nature and wiry Johnny with his glasses and high forehead had a bit of an intellectual air about him that got in the way of really coming across as a tough. Outsiders or not, they weren't above hanging out with the kids from school, who had fast cars and country houses where they could party on the weekends. In comparison to the native Argentines around them, the whole crowd had plenty of spending money, which they drank up, one bottle at a time.

Johnny steered the conversation back to the Mormons. That was how they had ended up at this random bar in La Lucila this day. A couple of Mormon "elders" in stiff suits and ties had invited them home to talk about their faith. It was just a lark for Johnny and

Bobby, but they sat and listened respectfully to talk about earning salvation through your ancestors and what appeared to them as other dubious ideas. Then they headed to a nearby bar to laugh it off and wash it down with the usual outpouring of alcohol.

Johnny kept circling back to the part about the afterlife. "I'm a materialist," he said to Bobby. "If you can't show me something I can see and touch, then I'm not gonna believe you." He took a thoughtful but tipsy draught from his glass. "Or, you can believe it Bobby. I'm just not gonna believe it with you."

Bobby nodded. This was what made them great friends. They could run around the city, getting drunk and chasing girls (more than once the combination of which had meant they'd had each other's backs in a fist fight), and in between the good times they would talk about death, life, and society. They talked about everything. And they went out a lot. Bobby said his home life was an "empty shell" and always had been. His parents were more interested in operas and parties than dealing with an extra-sensitive boy.

Johnny steered clear of his own house, too, and especially of his stepmother, Aida. She no longer made any secret of her dislike for him ever since Johnny's younger stepbrother contracted crabs at a brothel Johnny had taken him the summer before. Johnny felt sorry for his stepbrothers and two little half-sisters. Aida was tough with them too, but in a different way. Even without the constant conflict around Johnny's behavior, there was a lot of tension in the family.

Johnny had his own reasons to resent Aida for the sake of his own departed mother. Aida was the much younger sister of Mamá's best friend. The families had been close — Aida's parents were even Johnny's godparents. Though he had been little at the time, he remembered the tones Mamá and Marta used when they spoke about Aida. Marta refused even to speak her name and called her simply "the traitor." Aida was closer to Marta's age and they had also been friends. On some level, Johnny felt that just living with Aida was a betrayal of his mother. He stayed out of the house as much as possible and got into trouble while he was at it.

Johnny and Bobby in San Francisco

BY RAVEN

Two years later, Johnny and Bobby were spending the afternoon together on another continent. It was a chilly day in Golden Gate Park in San Francisco, but they had made a promise to climb a tree and not come down till they made a decision. In the distance, they could hear bongos and voices drifting over from Hippie Hill. They were tired of talking over the same points and tired of surprising passersby with unexpected greetings from above, so they kept quiet. Looking down at the limb below him, Johnny thought Bobby might even be asleep.

•••

It was two months since they'd first arrived in the Haight-Ashbury district of San Francisco. After high school, Johnny spent freshman year at Oklahoma State University. He studied petroleum engineering, as was expected of him, but managed not to work very hard at it. He did what he could for the anti-Vietnam War effort in the little Oklahoma town by helping start a branch of Students for a Democratic Society (SDS). It attracted no more than fifteen members but was nonetheless enough to warrant an FBI infiltrator that led to a threat of Johnny's deportation by U.S. immigration. In the summer, he saved money by working on an oil rig and bought a little red Chevy Monza. When he returned to school that fall, the first class on his schedule was calculus. Watching the professor write an impossibly long equation that stretched from one chalkboard to another around the room, Johnny realized he wouldn't be able to slide by anymore. He wouldn't last the week. He would either have to apply himself to this thing he didn't care about or drop out. The next morning, he sent a telegram to his father in La Paz.

"I'm done with school. I'm going to find myself," it said.

So Johnny got into his red Chevy and drove to Colorado, where Bobby went to school. His old friend was wilder and more lost than ever. Johnny sold the car in Denver, and from there the two hippies hitched a ride to San Francisco. It was 1966, the height of the flowering of the counterculture, and they had landed in its epicenter. The night they rolled in, they found friends and dropped acid. Johnny went to the Avalon Ballroom to see Jefferson Airplane, while Bobby stayed at their friend's in a fetal position till he came down from his trip. The next day, Johnny paid for a room in the Haight using the money from the car. From there on out, Bobby crashed with him or took surreptitious trips to and from Colorado as he pretended to go to college. They explored the city and tried whatever drugs they came across.

Haight street was flooded daily with newly arrived young people from across the country. People clustered on the sidewalks and in the park, day and night, constantly experimenting, partying, and playing. They tried on different modes of expression, from art making to imported spiritual practices. Music was central to every-thing for the hippies. Even non-musical Johnny went constantly to concerts and jam sessions or gathered with friends to play records at home. The big event of the summer of 1967 had been attending Jimi Hendrix's free concert in the park. The neighborhood was still abuzz with the shows he was playing at the Fillmore, so popular that they moved him to the top of the bill. Johnny missed both the Fillmore shows, but the concert in the park had been incred-ible and the crowd was ecstatic. That summer there had been a feeling of wild possibility. With so many people having their minds opened with drugs, art, and love, it seemed inevitable that the future would be an enlightened one. "The establishment" had lost its moral authority and conventions were crumbling. This led to an emboldened generation that poured youthful energy into anti-war and anti-racism activism, art, and fresh paradigms for society. The time for reform was over, and the only option seemed to be revolution, albeit only a cultural one.

•••

Meanwhile, Johnny and Bobby were still sitting in a tree in Golden Gate Park. They had climbed it on a whim, vowing not to come down until they made a decision about whether to stay in San Francisco or move on. They both wanted to stay, but the money from the car Johnny sold was almost gone. They had no jobs, no plans, and now the sun was getting low, with no solutions in sight.

"How about that cat on Stanyan Street?" said Bobby.

Johnny looked down again. So, he wasn't asleep. "That guy is far out," he replied skeptically. "I mean really far out."

Bobby agreed. They had met the guy just yesterday when Bobby went to look for an apartment. He'd pulled on his old school blazer and brushed his hair for the interview. Not only was his costume unnecessary, but the "cat" in question, the manager of the building, was the epitome of the Haight Street landlord. He opened the door wearing just a sarong. His large green eyes were at half-mast over a long reedy nose, like a mystic greyhound waking up from a nap. Before Bobby had fully crossed the threshold, he was offered a hit off a hash pipe.

Johnny arrived later, and between the hash and the acid they had all dropped, they couldn't remember when or how they agreed to the apartment. Still, Johnny had a key and a crumpled lease in his pocket, so apparently, he had signed on with that luxurious spaceman of a manager. Now, they'd either have to figure out how to pay for the place or would need to give up and leave town.

"Listen," said Johnny. "He said he was selling, and I saw for myself how many tabs of LSD he had in that bag. He had White Lightning, man. I think he has connections."

Bobby nodded.

"I mean, why don't we buy some from him and sell it?" said Johnny. "Why can't we be dealers?"

Bobby squinted up at him for a split second before he broke into a grin. He was glad to follow his friend anywhere, but this was right on. Immediately they laid their plans. The last bit of money from the Monza would buy the first round of acid. Johnny went on about the need people had for a new consciousness that only psychedelics would achieve. They would be entering into the social enterprise of turning people on. Souls would expand through cracks created by the ego-death of the acid trip. Besides, they both thought, with a little cash they would have a place to live and that would not hurt in terms of girls. The friends finally jumped down from the tree with a decision firmly in hand. They would stay in the Haight and deal acid.

Johnny and Bobby and the Diggers in the Haight

BY RAVEN

For a year, that's what Johnny and Bobby did. A few months in, they made connection with the guy at the top of the supply chain, and their profits went through the roof. One afternoon, Bobby paid for a new Volkswagen with the cash from just one deal. Another time, they were sitting around in a circle in the back room on Stanyan Street, smoking and tripping, when Bobby used a hundred-dollar bill to light their hash pipes. Right at that moment, a beautiful young model who was partying with them lay down and passed out. Bobby attributed it to her attachment to money. They were high on the hog (among other things) and they were happy to be creating the new free society while they were at it. Bobby and Johnny gradually saw less of one another. Bobby met a pretty redhead who also lived on the fringe and loved him as well as his money. Johnny dealt acid consistently but casually, with ample time for seeing concerts and running the Diggers' Free Store in the Haight.

He had been introduced to the Diggers after meeting one of their leaders, Peter Berg, one night at the Avalon Ballroom. Although the group claimed to be leaderless, it seemed to Johnny that Peter was basically at the helm. He was among a set of counterculture elders who'd come from the New York beatnik scene and from outlaw biker culture. He had access to thinkers like Timothy Leary, author of the legendary hippie maxim "turn on, tune in, and drop out," whom Peter took Johnny to meet one night at a house party. The Diggers were a loose bunch of activists and artists, advancing the social agenda of the hippie movement by living it. Some were affiliated with the San Francisco Mime Troupe, whose protest theater was full of satire and whimsy and, lately, inspired by the psychedelic experience. The central Digger tenet was to live the life you'd like to see. They wanted a world free from the quantifying values of capitalism, so they had a free store. They started a free medical clinic (the first of its kind), printed a free broadside full of psychedelic poetry and sketches, and passed out free food by the ton in Golden Gate Park. While it was true they were creatively inventing the society they wanted to live in, they were also filling the basic needs of the community around them when no one else was. When asked why they did it, they liked to respond enigmatically with the group's motto: "Diggers do."

As thousands of youths streamed into San Francisco, many became essentially homeless. Haight Street was sometimes four deep with young people just hanging out. Those not high on drugs were high on sudden freedom from the strict conventions of the

1950s. For the first time since the social liberalism of the Roaring 1920s, artistic and sexual expression had free reign in the streets and in their homes. That summer the influx multiplied because of a wave of mainstream media attention meant to warn small town America against the dangers of hippiedom. Instead, it acted like a signpost for youth looking for where the action was. Already by 1967, merchants and copycats capitalized on the influx, using peace and love ideology for advertising. The Diggers were inadvertent social workers in this stew of genuine social movement and general confusion. They were also rabble rousers, more libertine idealists than do-gooders. As a whole, they were in it to ride the chaos, even as they fed the hungry.

It was October, a warm month at the end of a chilly San Francisco summer, and Johnny sat behind the Free Store counter reading Hermann Hesse's *Siddhartha* in a moment of rest. Even though everything in the store was given away for free, there was still plenty to track and organize in donations. They mostly had books, records, and clothing, like any thrift store. They also had a pretty good turnover of musical instruments, art supplies, art, and even abandoned pets. There was a bowl on the counter where people could give or take money. "Free money," the sign read. The bowl was currently empty since the day before, when some Diggers had thrown an impromptu parade. They called the street theater happening "The Death of Money," and it was complete with a coffin carried by people in giant paper mâché animal heads. Naturally, they burned the coffin in the park, including the few dollars that were grabbed from the bowl. When Bobby walked into the store looking buzzed with excitement, Johnny assumed he'd stopped by to chat about the parade.

"I met Satan today, man."

Johnny could see he was visibly shaken. So it wasn't the Digger parade after all.

"Diane saw him too. Johnny, it was this red-headed guy, an incarnation. Too many souls flying around all these planes of existence, man. There's some really dark forces in this town right now," he said, looking around him as if there might be one or two lurking behind a clothing rack.

Bobby told him about the red-headed man he'd seen holding up a girl as she vomited into the street.

"He turned around and looked right at me and, I'm telling you, it chilled my bones."

Bobby continued. Later in the day his girlfriend reported a similar feeling when a guy asked her to get in a car with him. She saw the flashing red of the taillights as a sign — don't do it! Bobby asked her if the guy in the car had red hair. He had.

"It was the devil, Johnny."

Johnny listened sympathetically. He believed Bobby, or at least that this was his friend's genuine experience. Bobby had always had an intuitive side that Johnny was only just beginning to tune in to. He certainly didn't believe in Satan, or God either, but there was no doubt that the city was filled with vulnerable souls and people who preyed on them. He only had to look out the storefront window to see evidence. The effects of poverty and hard drugs were taking hold in the spaces originally freed up by the expansive hippie lifestyle. It was close to closing time anyway, so Johnny locked the door and the old friends sat in a diner across the street. They talked about the people they knew, the old days in Argentina, and the tragedies of American society and hippie subculture, each in turn. The excitement of the brave-new-world had been replaced with the grim exhilaration of living through what now seemed like the end-of-days — maybe for the hippie movement and definitely for the scene in the Haight.

The Inflection Point
The Gospel of Matthew

BY JUAN-LORENZO

I held the memory of my Mirror Experience close to my heart. I didn't know how to apply it to my life but felt certain that if I kept my eye to the prism, I would find a way. Through my vision, I'd seen the things I had not been: not kind, not sincere, not even conscious of the way I affected those around me. I particularly thought about a period a few months earlier when I had rented two different apartments in order to have two separate girlfriends at once. The Mirror Experience had shown me that I could not continue to live my life out of my own ego, but I didn't have the tools to find another way forward. I was in a crisis of my own making; it was my assessments, judgments, and willfulness that had led me to the dead end revealed to me by my Mirror Experience. I knew there had to be a different foundation to my life, but I did not know how to proceed. Not knowing where else to look, I turned to the Zen Center in San Francisco. There I practiced emptying myself on the inside.

As it happened, a few nights after that day on the patio, I had gone to see a movie with a friend. It was an Italian film with subtitles, called *The Gospel According to St. Matthew*, directed by Pier Paolo Pasolini. It was beautifully shot in black and white, with long dense silences populated by nothing but the actor's expressive gaze and dialogue inserted directly from the Scriptures. It showed Jesus the prophet and revolutionary. His dark intensity was broken only by his delight in the innocence of children. Something in the film intrigued me, and I right afterwards I got my hands on a copy of the New Testament.

Soon, I found myself sitting on my couch with a Bible in my hand, alone in my apartment once again. It was a crisp morning and I'd already had my breakfast of brown rice and soy sauce — essentially the same meal I ate three times a day. I opened to Matthew and read the story I already knew from the half-hearted Catholic upbringing of my boyhood. Jesus, born under a star, escaping death at the hands of Herod, being tempted in the wilderness: a litany of events aligning with prophecies from even more ancient days. Then Jesus starts preaching and healing. He teaches about compassion and faith. He tells parables.

"Do not be worried about the food and drink you
need in order to stay alive, or about clothes for

your body.... Look at the birds: they do not plant seeds... Look how the wildflowers grow: they do not work or make clothes for themselves. But I tell you that not even King Solomon with all his wealth had clothes as beautiful as one of these flowers....Your Father in heaven knows that you need these things. Instead, be concerned above everything else with the Kingdom of God and with what he requires of you, and all else will be added unto you."

As I read this simple beautiful passage, I felt another ineffable shift. Time settled in around itself, into my body and the space around me. The words on the page became living, radiant things. They leapt up and shouted directly into my soul. "Look how the flowers grow," I read; but also, I *heard*. "He will provide for you" rang out deep inside me. I wondered about this Kingdom of God that invited my soul to such profound response. Calm, centered, but flying inside, I kept reading. Several passages later, it happened again.

"The Kingdom of Heaven is like this. A man happens to find a treasure hidden in a field. He covers it up again and is so happy that he goes and sells everything he has, and then goes back and buys that field. Also, the Kingdom of Heaven is like this. A man is looking for fine pearls, and when he finds one that is unusually fine, he goes and sells everything he has, and buys that pearl."

All these words from the Bible felt deeply personal. They were *for* me, they were *about* me, and they *freed me* from myself. Their message wasn't about literal heaven, or even about the enlightenment of Buddhist tradition. It was a description of how to be close to Holy Mystery while still in the flawed human state we are in. They were a directive to surrender control to the sacred, even to the point of owning nothing. It was a description of the path of the *sadhu*, the Hindu wandering ascetic.

I put down the book and looked around me. The words were still glowing in my heart and it gave my surroundings an extraordinary clarity. My accumulated books and furniture seemed utterly extraneous. So did the roof over my head. Then I thought about my stash of bills rolled up under the sink in a shoe box. It was a lot of money, but it no longer felt attached to me. I actually didn't own it any longer; it was just something I had. I took out the money, counted it, and divided it into two paper bags. I took a walk, ate another meal, and later that night when an acquaintance dropped in to say hello I handed him one of those bags. The next morning, another friend came by to return a book, and I gave him the other bag. Neither friend was close enough in my life for me to even remember their names now, but I do remember vividly how shocked they were. Each of them protested and we laughed a lot. But finally, they accepted the money and walked out the door with it. In today's money, it was $60,000. For me, though, it was just the first natural step towards a new life that had been revealed to me, first in the Mirror Experience and then through the Inflection Point brought about by those living passages in the Gospel of St. Matthew.

Johnny Goes to Shanti and then the Banana Patch

BY RAVEN

In the next few weeks, Johnny moved into action or, rather, inaction. He cleared out whatever furniture he had in his apartment. He painted it white and turned it into an essentially public space. People could stop in at any time and sit *zazen*, Zen meditation, with him. There were various spiritual seekers rolling through the city of San Francisco in those days, and a couple of young American *sadhus* landed in the backyard. They were young men with long beards who cooked and ate over a fire outside, following a vow they had made to never go indoors. Johnny meditated, and throughout the day and night he read the few books he hadn't given away. He read the Zen text, *The Gateless Gate*, and his recently acquired New Testament, and he continued to eat an austere diet of brown rice and soy sauce. Now the door to the apartment was always open.

By giving away first his money and then his possessions and personal space, Johnny was following the inspiration he received from the passages in the Gospel of St. Matthew. He wanted to expose himself as much as possible to the direct influence of Holy Mystery, so much so that he felt compelled not to touch money at all. Johnny gave up all interaction with currency and trusted that when his bag of rice ran out he would somehow be provided for.

"Be concerned above all else with the Reign of God and with what it requires of you, and all else will be added unto you." This beautiful bit of scripture became his guiding light.

•••

Johnny was sitting on the front steps, thinking about his impending move, now only days away. He had paid at the rent for his apartment through the end of the month and no further. In the process of making his home into a *zendo*, he'd already accomplished everything he needed in order to leave. It was painted and clean. He had nothing to pack, as he no longer had any possessions beyond what he could carry. His problem was something different. He had no idea where he would go.

Then one day Johnny broke into a smile when he saw his best friend Bobby walking down the street towards him.

"I heard about your *zendo*, Johnny," Bobby said. "Far out."

Bobby took a seat with Johnny on the stoop as Johnny told him everything, from the Mirror Experience to the Inflection Point to giving away all his money and the weeks that had followed. They were joined by someone stopping in to sit *zazen* at the house, a young man from Wyoming who called himself Indigo.

"I only know that I am not supposed to touch money," Johnny told Bobby and Indigo. "I guess when the end of the month rolls around, I'll just start walking."

Bobby looked concerned, but he was also excited. "This is radical, man. You were *told* to let go, and now you're *going* to let go. And you *look* different too." Bobby cocked his shaggy head to the side. "Your eyes look different. Brighter, man."

Indigo spoke up. "Listen, Johnny," he said. "If you don't know where you're going, why don't you come with us? There's this Zen Buddhist retreat center up in the Santa Cruz mountains called Shanti. We have a gig up there looking after the place for room and board. All the *dharma* talks you want would be for free. You could just join in."

Johnny felt the next step in the journey being revealed, and before he had even asked who "we" were or how "we" would get there, he said, "Yes! I'll bring my bag of rice."

As it turned out, "they" would get there in a VW van. It pulled up two days later as Johnny walked out of the Stanyan Street apartment for the last time.

Inside the van were the lanky Indigo; a stocky, even younger fellow named Willie; and a girl with a halo of frizzy blonde hair who introduced herself as Naomi. They were all heavily into yoga and sang Sanskrit chants about Shiva all the way up to the mountain. The redwood and eucalyptus trees became taller and the temperature dropped ten degrees as the bus slowly churned up a winding road and through the gates of the retreat center. The trio of friends were new as caretakers. But the three had spent some time at the center before. They showed Johnny around the meditation and dining halls and explained how to care for the shrine.

•••

Johnny's duties in looking after the grounds only took a few hours out of the day. As the weeks went by, he developed a routine of filling the remaining hours with meditation and study. He now included *pranayama*, the meditative yogic breathwork that he was learning from his new friends. Indigo, Willie, and Naomi hung out with other people at the center and practiced a lot of *asanas*, the physical poses of Yoga. They sometimes went down to the Santa Cruz boardwalk or further along the coast to Big Sur, but Johnny mostly stayed put and spent his time focused on his own spiritual practices. One afternoon, Indigo approached him to talk about their wish to lead a more "natural life." The group had a plan to go to Hawaii to a community they knew about, where they could build their own houses and live off the land. He said that if Johnny would share with him the contacts he had for buying acid, the three friends would pool their money, invest in one big deal, and buy tickets to the island. Johnny thought about it. Being grateful for the ride and arrangement at Shanti, he agreed. Indigo and Willie took off in their VW headed for the Haight. When they came back, they had not three, but four tickets to the island. Johnny was surprised and, again, grateful. Two months after arriving at Shanti, he was going to Maui.

Their destination was a place near Lahaina called the Banana Patch. The island was unbelievably lush and verdant, and the Patch was no exception. It was, in fact, a tract of cultivated land, a banana farm belonging to a man named David Joseph. David was an eccentric old bootlegger who'd married a native Hawaiian wife and welcomed hippies with open arms. He loved to build rickety structures out of driftwood, pallets, and discarded windows. The young people of the counterculture happily helped him build them, then lived in them. There were two rules for the commune: "Don't strike your brother" and "Don't touch the bananas." Other than that, the old man basically left "the children" alone.

When Johnny arrived, there were twenty-odd shacks dotting the land and a cultivated garden. Occupying them were a smattering of young couples and small groups, a few with little children. It was a quiet place with a fluid itinerant population who lived out a philosophy of peace and were usually vegetarian. Johnny had no problem finding a wooden platform that someone before him had built and abandoned. The weather was so temperate that he seldom used his tent, preferring to sleep in a sleeping bag under the stars.

Johnny passed many months at the Banana Patch. He saw numbers of people come and go, and though everyone was friendly he didn't form any lasting connections. He lived off the wild fruits of the island and the generosity of the other hippies who gave him both rice and a wide berth. As much time as he could muster, he devoted to reading and the disciplines of yoga and meditation. Still, there were hours of each day that felt incredibly long and tedious. Without much food to give him energy, Johnny spent most of his time resting in the shade of banana trees. It was a life of stark simplicity that contained the seeming contradiction of strict discipline and plenty of non-doing.

Johnny had unequivocally left his old life behind. He felt himself searching steadily for a new way forward, and he knew he hadn't found it yet, though he knew he was on the way.

• • •

One day, several months into their stay, Indigo came to Johnny's platform to say goodbye. He and Naomi were leaving for another island. They wanted to know if Johnny intended to stay at the Banana Patch and how things were going for him. It had been weeks since they'd seen each other.

"Are you going to stick around the Patch for a while, Johnny? I mean, are you getting any closer to enlightenment?" Indigo was joking, but he seemed to want to know, just in case. The two young men got into a conversation about what enlightenment would even mean for a post-industrial person of the 20th century.

"It's just that I've discovered that I don't know anything at all," said Johnny. "Everything I thought I knew back in the Haight was actually my mind and body making excuses to keep me away from my soul. Back before I left the mainland, I had a couple of experiences that showed me that I don't have to know what I'm supposed to do now anyway. It's possible to receive knowledge and be guided when you need it."

"But if you ask me," Johnny continued, what I have been doing out here in Maui, is unfurling my sails. If you have a sailboat, you have to open the sail. And you have to be able to guide the sail in such a way that it will catch the wind. And if you can do that, then the sailboat will move. I'm forming my being into something with the ability to catch the wind. All of this is ultimately about the wind, which is always there. Always blowing. The wind is Spirit. It's *Prana, Ruah, Chi.*"

So Indigo and Naomi left, but Johnny continued to live among the banana trees and work on his ability to hear that guidance if it should come again. Nine months passed before he felt an impulse strong enough that it felt to him like a directive. It told him to get up and walk all the way around the island. So Johnny set out. It was a journey of about ten days at the easy pace he chose. He carried on his back his rice-pot, his bag of brown rice, and his sleeping bag, all he had when he'd first arrived. As he walked, Johnny absorbed the breathtaking beauty of Maui. The coast was an unbroken palette of pure turquoise water, white sand, and jewel-toned birds and flowers. It was dotted with waterfall coves and heralded by the spouts and glistening fins of marine mammals offshore. Johnny had to be careful to find and ration water, but otherwise the island was gentle with him. Five days into his trek, he was walking along the water's edge when he noticed a figure emerge from the trees across the sand. As he got closer, the man started to wave his arms and run towards him. Johnny stopped and watched, more curious than alarmed. When the figure came clearly into view, Johnny laughed from sheer surprise. It was Bobby Aguirre.

• • •

Johnny and Bobby spent the remainder of that day catching up while resting in the shade of some palm trees. Bobby had heard through the grapevine in San Francisco that Johnny was in Maui at the Banana Patch. Johnny had flown over just to say hello and found out that Johnny was walking around the island. They were both amazed that Bobby's relatively random path had led him straight to Johnny along a shoreline that is 120 miles long. It seemed like another confirmation to Johnny that he was walking closely with Holy Mystery.

Bobby talked excitedly about his plan to sell macrobiotic foods on the island. He was getting a big shipment of brown rice, and planned to send for his wife and baby son once he was established. Johnny noticed some fatal flaws in the plan. For example, Bobby had developed no distribution system and wanted to serve a customer base that was infamous for having no money. Still, Johnny hoped the trip would lead Bobby away from dealing drugs, so he kept quiet. That night the two friends slept in the sand at the edge of the jungle, and the next day they continued together Johnny's journey along the rim of the sea. After another night in the sand, Bobby said goodbye and trekked inland to hitch a ride on the road to Lahaina.

•••

Three days later, as Johnny finished his circumambulation of the island and trudged back up to his platform at the Banana Patch, he felt like his feet were made of lead. He fell asleep before sundown, and when he woke the next morning he had a fever. It was the first time he'd been sick since he began his macrobiotic diet. It turned out to be a bad flu, lasting from that week into the next. After the fever broke, he remained under the weather for another full week. People from the commune brought him water and rice. A friend dropped off a book for him by J. G. Bennett, the esotericist, about a spiritual movement called *Subud*. Because *Subud* had roots in mystical Islam, the book spoke a lot about surrender to God. Johnny was intrigued by this and noticed that in the back of the book there was a contact address for someone in Honolulu. He thought no more of it, but he kept the book.

When his health improved, Johnny set to work to find a way off the island. It had become clear to him that his time on Maui was at an end. The walk around the island had confirmed this, and recently his pranayama breathwork had been ending in hyperventilation. He knew through the responses of his body that he'd gone as far as he could on his own. He needed a teacher to get any further with his meditation. He'd heard that Satchidananda, the yogic teacher from India, was living on Honolulu, and he decided that connecting with the guru would be the next step.

However, Johnny could hardly leave an island without buying a ticket by air or sea, and that involved having to make and then spend money. He found out where he could get work as a day laborer and spent just one day picking pineapples in the sun. When he was handed his pay, he saw that there was just enough for the ticket he needed, but something in him felt very uneasy about spending that money. He turned and handed it to one of the other laborers and walked back to the Banana Patch, not sure what else to do. A couple of days later, a friend on the commune walked up and handed him a plane ticket to Honolulu. Word had gotten around about his dilemma, and someone had taken up a collection. For the third time, a door had opened to bring him further down the road.

Johnny in Honolulu

Johnny squinted across the tarmac in Honolulu at a sign on the control tower that read "Aloha" in huge curly letters. He made his way through the airport, carrying his usual backpack and sleeping bag. His simple clothes hung off a body grown very thin. His black hair and beard were long, and his skin was burnished a dark caramel brown. After so long in the elements, Johnny's senses were stunned by the sterile hubbub of the airport. Everything seemed too bright and too smooth. The tourists were too fat, their matching his-and-her muumuus and leis seemed so strange. He stood in the atrium looking around until he realized that the tourists had a similar stunned and alarmed look on their faces, and it was because of the sight of him!

Johnny shouldered his pack and made his way through the city. He found a bar and cafe known as a hippie haunt, where he inquired about the whereabouts of Satchidananda.

"You just missed him, brother," said a towheaded surfer with no shirt. "He left for San Francisco day before yesterday. They say he got word in a vision that the kids out there really need enlightenment these days. Heroin, man." The guy shook his head and turned back to the bar. "Peace."

For the second time that day, Johnny felt a little stunned. Hadn't Holy Mystery just perfectly led him here to meet this teacher? What had gone wrong? He asked around for a place to lay his head that night and was told about a cave he could walk to in the mountain above the city — the famous Diamond Head overlooking Honolulu. That night Johnny crouched at the edge of the cave to watch the sun go down. He thought about the string of synchronicities that had led him there and took out his Bible and read again the passages from St. Matthew that had so moved him. He had put such absolute faith in the way things would unfold, it seemed impossible that the teacher he sought had left to go to the place Johnny had given up everything to get away from. As the last of the color on the horizon faded to dark, he lit a candle stub and lost himself in his book about *Subud*. Suddenly, he remembered the Honolulu address printed as a contact in the back of that book. Having nowhere else to go, he resolved he would walk there in the morning.

•••

The address was in a suburb of Honolulu called Ala Moana, and when he arrived it was still late morning. Conscious of how wild and weird he must look, he made an attempt to finger comb his long hair, and then gave up and rang the bell, book in hand. A heavily pregnant woman answered the door, two little children peeking around her house dress.

"Excuse me. Ma'am," he said, "I've just come from some time camping on Maui, and I'm here to learn about *Subud.*" He held up the book and smiled hopefully. To his surprise, the woman smiled back and invited him inside.

She introduced herself as Emily. She had a London accent, lank blonde hair, and a lively face. She told him that her husband, Maartin, was at work at the Bishop Museum and would be back for dinner.

"Yes," she said, responding to his questions, "we are *Subud* members. Would you like to take a shower?" It sounded more like a suggestion than a question.

She handed him a towel and turned back to the children, who were running around, excited about the unexpected visitor. After Johnny cleaned up, she left him with some tea to wait for her husband to come home from work. Johnny sat down to dinner wearing new clothes. The clothes were his now, as Emily had made it clear that his old ones were going in the trash. Sensing that it was time to break his macrobiotic diet, Johnny ate what the family ate — a mash of potatoes, vegetables, and sausage. After dinner, he sat with Maartin in some chairs outside to enjoy the twilight. His host was prematurely bald and less animated than his wife, though with a grave attentiveness that made him easy to talk to. He spoke with a slight Dutch accent and seemed delighted to talk about *Subud.* Johnny learned it was related to Islam and had been founded by an Indonesian man named Muhammad Subuh Sumohadiwidjojo, affectionately known as Bapak. He already knew from the book that it entailed seeking and receiving guidance from God through a freewheeling spiritual practice called the *latihan*.

•••

During the weeks to come, Emily and Maartin would feed and house him, and he would accompany them to *Subud* gatherings. The latihan was a leaderless group exercise. Participants were separated by gender, as in the Islamic tradition of the founder, and then simply stood together in a room until they felt inspired by God to vocalize, sing, or move. Bapak was due to arrive, and when he did, Maartin and Emily took Johnny to meet him.

The founder was a small, wizened Indonesian man with a ready smile. Johnny found him to be genuine and unassuming. He soon realized that hosting and educating seekers was a part of the *Subud* tradition, and he felt very lucky indeed. Johnny helped the family repair things around the house and he kept up his meditation and yoga practices, though in a much more relaxed way. One afternoon, feeling more energetic than he had in some time, he decided to go for a run. In less than a single block, his depleted body stopped him short with a painful stitch in his side. He realized that he had a way to go to rejoin society, if indeed that was what he was ultimately called to do.

The Running and Anointing Experience

BY JUAN-LORENZO

The family was sleeping, and the neighborhood outside was quiet. My eyes opened and I found myself completely awake. There it was again, that shift in reality, a subtle but unmistakable change in the air. I knew it was another sacred time-out-of-time.

I felt myself get out of bed and stand in the darkened room. I didn't *decide* to get out of bed. I had no *reason* and no conscious *will* to do it. It just *happened*. My limbs shifted weight and lifted me until I was balancing on my bare feet in the moonlight. My heart skipped a beat. Was I out of control? Surely not being in command over my own body was the very definition of out of control. I paused on the tail of that skipped heartbeat and looked inward. Was this ok? Was this a good thing?

It was. It was good. And I sensed if it became too much my free will remained intact and standing off to the side. I could withdraw my consent at any moment and return to my usual state of mind. So, for the first time that night, I said "yes".

With that "yes," my body glided into motion again. I put on clothes and laced up my shoes. I walked out the sliding door and into the sleeping suburban street and began to run. And what a run it was! I ran past the corner where I had been stopped by a stitch in my side the day before. I ran another block and another. My body moved effortlessly, like an animal in the chase; each sinew, bone, and muscle acting together in fluid harmony. They carried me down one street after another. I felt no pain and no effort. And my heart was rejoicing. I came to know then that there was something much deeper and wiser than myself that could move me. I still wasn't certain if I believed in God in the way my *Subud* hosts now did and my Catholic mother had.

Nevertheless, my body, with the assent of my mind, was engaged in a separate and powerful conversation with some unseen force of wholeness. As my legs moved and the soft air bellowed in and out of my lungs, I felt a clear invitation from Holy Mystery. It was an invitation for me to become part of the world in a new way, a way that served something higher than myself. I felt myself slow to an easy walk. In my heart, a simple question resounded: "Will you serve?"

"Yes," I said. Again, I gave my assent, just as I had in the Haight.

...

My walk continued, unfurling through the quiet night. I found myself approaching a graveyard. It was a Japanese cemetery, with gentle but meticulous landscaping and narrow headstones with vertical inscriptions. As I walked among them, the fear came back to me. I had given up control of my destination. If I came across an empty grave, and my body climbed into it, what then? Was I ready for death? If this was what it meant to serve, was I truly willing? Again, I paused and looked inside for a response. Again, the answer was "yes."

I didn't climb into a grave that night; my steps led me out of the graveyard. Gradually regaining my normal sense of volition, I walked back to the house and my bed. That night I slept a sleep so deep that I learned a new meaning for the word "profound." I didn't speak to the family I was living with, or to anyone else for that matter, about my experience the night before. It wasn't necessary. I knew, and I knew that I knew. That was enough.

...

Some days later, I went on another walk, this one ordinary in every way. The weather on Oahu is always close to perfect. I was wearing the sandals, pants cut into shorts, and cotton shirt Maartin had given me to replace the tattered clothes I'd arrived in. That day, rain clouds were gathering in the distance for one of the brief tropical showers that blesses the island every afternoon. I walked out of the neighborhood and along a local stream, taking my time and mulling things over.

It was clear to me that my ascetic period was over. I was also clear, with an inner certainty, that I needed to be part of a spiritual tradition of some kind. Because of the recent strange and wonderful experience of running with the spirit, I knew I was being guided, but I couldn't have recognized that what I experienced was "God." I only knew it was good, it was big, and it had called my name.

As I strolled, I decided to put the question directly to that Holy Mystery. "What if I became Hindu?" I said. "I love the Bhagavad Gita and Patanjali's Aphorisms. I love doing yoga."

As I formed the thought completely in my head and offered it up, I heard, or rather felt, an immediate response. "Yes, you could do that. But...."

I kept walking. After a while, another thought came to me, and again I offered it up. "What if I became Buddhist? I love Zen meditation, the story of Siddhartha, and I resonate deeply with the Four Noble Truths."

Again, the answer came clearly. "Yes, you could do that. But...."

I stopped walking. I sensed a new, very difficult question being directly addressed to me.

"What would be the hardest thing for you to do?"

The answer to that was obvious: Catholic Christianity—that arcane and often oppressive system I had rejected out of hand many years before. I had discounted anything of worth in it and, anyway, I didn't believe in that kind of God. The belief that a man who was hung on a cross to die is God? It was an absurd idea, but I took a deep breath. "Ok," I said. "I hope you know what you're doing. I don't see it. But I will do it. I say 'yes.'"

With that, I felt an astounding sensation move over me. It felt like a literal anointing, like oil was cascading over my body. The sensation started at the crown of my head and poured down to my feet. With it came a sense of otherworldly peace that penetrated my entire being. Later, I would identify it with a phrase from the letters of Paul that describes "the peace of God, which surpasses all understanding." This indeed was a peace that was of God and at the same time part of me. It came with my full "yes" to follow this Holy Mystery, even into that religion I had most strenuously resisted.

I had practiced this radical spiritual consent when, in my running, I'd let my body be moved by the unknowable, and even more so when, in the graveyard, I'd allowed for my own possible death. My running experience spoke to me about a way of moving through the world in connection to Holy Mystery. This connection would allow me to use my life to serve something greater than myself. My yes to death had in fact been a yes to life, including its impermanence and its imperfection. With the sensation of being washed with warm holy oil, my "fiat" was made real. Then and there, I resolved to find out everything I could about Catholic Christianity, now with my heart open to its faith and its poetry. I knew I would need to put my critical, judging self aside long enough to discover where the sacred resided in the religious tradition I had rejected so vehemently and so long. I would become a Christian Catholic, whatever that meant.

Juan Carlos Takes a New Name

BY RAVEN

Back in college after his long spiritual quest in Hawaii, Johnny was sitting at the Catholic Student Center at the University of Texas in Austin. He was reading intently, his psychology textbooks and scholarly journals spread around him. The second time around, he loved college. Intervening life experiences had given him a real thirst for knowledge, and he soaked up his studies like a sponge. On this day, however, his course books sat on the table untouched. Instead, he was reading from a slim volume entitled *New Monastic Communities*. It featured friends of his at St. Benedict's Farm, a co-ed religious community that seemed more like a commune than a monastery. Whenever he could, he went to work alongside them and to chat with his friends long into the warm East Texas night. The monks lived under the Rule of St. Benedict and took vows of poverty, chastity, and obedience, though they chose to make their own path on the fringes of Catholic tradition. So many young religious people in the early seventies were actively experimenting with the Farm's lifestyle that it had already been identified as a "new monastic movement."

After leaving Hawaii and spending some months in Bolivia, Johnny had enrolled for one semester back at Oklahoma State. There he'd been in a loving relationship with a woman seven years his senior — the single mother of two little girls. The relationship came to an end when Johnny returned from a visit with his stepbrother, Nano, who was then enrolled at the University of Texas. Johnny had fallen in love with the culture of Austin, which combined cowboy, Mexican-American, and hippie sensibilities into a laid-back haven for intellectuals and outcasts. The scrub-brush hill country around the city was laced with spring-fed rivers and streams, perfect for a swim after a sweltering hike.

When Johnny transferred to the University of Texas, he parted ways with his girlfriend and her daughters and decided to discover a more permanent path for his life before becoming romantically involved again. He felt open to meeting his soul mate, but he was also open to remaining celibate and leading a focused spiritual life as a single Catholic. It was a result of his "anointing experience" in Honolulu for him to put judgement on the back burner and allow the goodness and truth of what he had once deemed "empty of the sacred" to disclose itself to him in the Catholicism he now practiced.

• • •

After that anointing, Johnny had felt a strong call to be reconciled with his family. While in Bolivia, he'd stayed with his father, stepmother, and siblings. He took care to make a formal apology to his parents, especially for the grief he'd caused them during his high school years. They accepted his apology. He also shared with them his spiritual stories, from the mirror experience, to running with the spirit through the night streets of Honolulu. They were less understanding about that and sent him to see a psychiatrist. The doctor confirmed their suspicions that Johnny was mentally unstable. Luckily, he also saw a Jesuit priest as a spiritual advisor. He was a kind man who understood Johnny's story from a spiritual perspective and was able to convince the psychiatrist of Johnny's sanity. Johnny had immersed himself in Catholicism with an intentionally open mind and decided to revert to the name he had been given in baptism: Juan Carlos. He let himself be moved by whatever truth lay hidden in the Mass and the rituals he vaguely remembered from his boyhood. It was a time of intense exploration of the spiritual traditions of Christianity.

Johnny, now Juan Carlos once again, reconnected with his conventional family, but he was still a radical at heart. He visited Junior, his older brother, who was now married and well-along in a career in petroleum engineering, just like their father. When Junior gave him some of his own clothes to wear, Johnny took them into the street and gave them to the homeless. Junior was not pleased. Though it was difficult to articulate at the time, the act reflected a growing alignment of his hippie social values with Christ's teaching about serving the poor. He was beginning to understand Christianity in the light of social justice.

Having never received the Sacrament of Confirmation, Johnny decided it would be a natural next step in his deepening relationship with the Catholic faith. When it came time to choose a new name in the tradition of confirmation, he chose the name "Lorenzo," after the early Christian martyr, Saint Lawrence. The saint had been a deacon in the early Church of Rome and served as the treasurer in charge of giving and receiving alms. When the Emperor Valerian decided to persecute the new religion by confiscating its property and executing its leaders, Lawrence quickly gave away everything of value to the poor. When he was called to hand over the wealth of the Church, he presented a collection of beggars, widows, and the disabled, saying, "These are the riches of the Church."

At his Confirmation, Juan Carlos would change his name for the final time. In twenty-two years, he'd gone from Juan Carlos to Charly to Johnny back to Juan Carlos, and now he finally chose to call himself Juan-Lorenzo. Taking the new name was a symbolic gesture. Like all symbols, it manifested a meaning that worked quietly in the background in the years to come as he looked for his calling in the world.

Juan-Lorenzo Meets Sarah

BY RAVEN

Juan-Lorenzo looked up from his book and gazed out at the quiet lobby of the Catholic Student Center just as a young woman walked in. She came down the stairs from the street and stood near the entranceway, looking around and hugging her books to her chest. She had short curly hair and was fairly tall, with a graceful bearing. Usually, the priest at the Center was close at hand to greet new students, but when he didn't appear Juan-Lorenzo offered to show her around. She returned his offer with a warm intelligent smile. The Catholic Student Center was housed in a humble modern building whose main feature was a small auditorium, populated with folding chairs and used for Sunday services. There was a basement kitchen, a small chapel, some office areas, and the little

65

library where he had been studying. As they walked past his table of books, the woman reached down and picked up *New Monastic Communities*.

"Oh, are you familiar with this?" Juan-Lorenzo asked. "These are friends of mine."

"Well, I've read about the new monastic movement. But I've never experienced one," she said, looking at a black-and-white photo of some of the simple monastic buildings on the back cover of the book.

The two chatted about his time at St. Benedict's Farm as they walked around the Student Center. Their conversation was free and easy, and Juan-Lorenzo felt a growing excitement about meeting her. By the time they concluded their tour, he was paying close attention to that feeling.

"So, are you new to Austin?"

"I just arrived Tuesday, actually. I live with my sister off campus, but other than that, I haven't seen much."

"I could show you around, if you like. I know a cool old beer-garden near the Capitol where we could have a beer."

"I'd like that," she said, and she wrote her name and number for him on a sheet from her notebook: *Sarah*.

Juan-Lorenzo stared after her when she'd gone. He didn't know what it was he was feeling, but from all his experiences with Holy Mystery he knew that he didn't have to understand in order to trust his intuition. He had met the person destined to be his wife. Later that afternoon, his cousin and roommate, Guido, came home to find him sitting on the couch, staring at the sheet of paper.

"What have you got there?" said Guido.

"It's the number for a girl I met today named Sarah. If I call her, I'm going to marry her."

"A girl who just gave you her number?" Guido asked, laughing and shaking his head. "You are crazy, man."

But Juan-Lorenzo was already dialing the number.

• • •

Their first date turned into a story they would tell for the rest of their lives. They went to Shultz' Biergarten and sat at a picnic table under an ancient looking oak tree. They drank and chatted over the strains of an electric blues band playing on a tiny plywood stage. Juan-Lorenzo learned that Sarah had grown up in a large family from a small city on the Gulf Coast in Mississippi. She was a sophomore and had just transferred from a small Catholic college close to her home. She talked about the eye-opening summer before, when she'd lived with her sister in New York City. She spoke very warmly about her parents and seven siblings back home, six of them sisters. She missed them, she said, but she'd come to Austin to discover a wider world than Mississippi could ever offer. Sometimes Sarah seemed like a very young, naïve girl. Other times, she was clearly an intelligent grown woman with a strong grasp of her own foundational beliefs.

When they left Schultz', they dropped in on a friend of Juan-Lorenzo's who was a jazz musician, to chat and listen to jazz records. After a while, Sarah mentioned that her new contact lenses were bothering her and went to take them out, but before long her eyes were in so much pain she couldn't open them at all. With one hand cupped over her eyes, she turned to Juan-Lorenzo and said she would "need to get to the university clinic now." The date concluded with a trust-walk, as Juan-Lorenzo led her by the hand across campus in total blindness. It was a silly incident, but as time went on it felt providential. It set the stage for a deeper trust that would grow quickly and surely into a life-long partnership. They kept seeing each other, and soon enough, they were simply "Juan-Lorenzo and Sarah."

He got to know her family on a trip to Mississippi for Thanksgiving. They were a large Catholic tribe, with very little money and a lot of religious fervor. They were short on practicality and big on joy, which came out, often as not, in singing and dancing. Most importantly for Juan-Lorenzo, he recognized a strong maternal culture in the women. Sarah and her mother and sisters were very warm and nurturing. As he got to know her, he only felt affirmation that his first impulse had been a true one.

···

A few weeks into dating, Sarah came over one night and told Juan-Lorenzo that she was pregnant by another man. She had just been to the doctor and confirmed it. The father was a former boyfriend, a friend of her sister's that she'd known from a previous visit and had been seeing casually for the first few days after arriving in Austin. The very night before she'd met Juan-Lorenzo at the Catholic Student Center, she had been on a date with the young man and had chosen to give up her virginity to him. Juan-Lorenzo took the surprise pregnancy in stride and offered to support her whatever she chose to do. Sarah was agnostic at the time, but given her new relationship with Juan-Lorenzo, her beliefs about abortion, and the prevalent social stigmas and expectations, there was only one choice she really considered. She declared she would have the baby and give it up for adoption.

A few months later, when Sarah was just seven months

along, she went into labor prematurely. Juan-Lorenzo immediately took her to the hospital, but the labor turned out to be a slow process with lots of time waiting. Juan-Lorenzo sat with her, talking together between contractions, and passing the hours. They chatted softly, conscious of the other laboring women in the same large room, separated from them only by curtains. The nurse came and went and let them know that if the contractions didn't speed up in another hour or so they would administer a drug to help her along. Juan-Lorenzo held Sarah's hand and marveled at how unafraid she seemed. She took the pain as a matter of course and had settled into the slow rhythm of waiting and bearing up with a gentle endurance. The wait had been so long that Sarah's parents had time to drive eight hours from Mississippi and were already settled in the waiting room — along with three of her sisters, the father of the baby, Robert, and his new girlfriend!

Juan-Lorenzo realized Sarah had been looking at him thoughtfully, and he smiled at her. "What is it, Sarah?" he asked her.

"It's just funny. You're in here, and my family is out there. I always thought I would want Mama and Daddy with me in a moment like this. I mean, I couldn't imagine it any other way. But I'm just realizing I don't. I'm glad you're here with me instead."

"This is exactly where I want to be. You know there's nothing else more important for me."

She looked at him for another long moment. "I'm just realizing what it means to me to have you here. And what you mean to me." She leaned over and kissed him.

Sarah's mother and sister eventually moved quietly into the small room, and Juan-Lorenzo went out into the corridor. He paused and leaned against the wall, breathing deeply. He had known since the day they met that he and Sarah were going to get married. They had talked about raising the baby together instead of adoption, but they had decided against it and had made space for the birth without any more talk of marriage. Now, Juan-Lorenzo grinned. He finally *felt* it. Sarah did really want to be with him too. The time was right, and he rushed outside. In another half hour he was back at her bedside with a little ring in his hand. He had driven down to the stalls selling trinkets and imports that lined the main drag in front of the university and purchased a little silver twisted-wire ring from Mexico.

"Sarah, I love you so much. Will you marry me?" he said, holding up the ring at the side of her cot.

She didn't hesitate. She said, "Yes."

The doctor returned with the medicine and within a couple hours Sarah had delivered a baby boy. She named him Robert, after his father. He was very small, but since he cried before they took him away to the nursery she thought all was well and went to sleep without concern. Little Robert was too premature for the technology of the day, however. In the morning, the doctor told them the baby did not survive the night. Sarah cried, and together she and Juan-Lorenzo offered up prayers for the tiny baby. A few days later, they held a small funeral at the Catholic cemetery. Sarah and Juan-Lorenzo had thought the child would go away to a life with new parents, most likely never to be seen again. Instead, he had passed from this world in a way that felt like his life was never fully meant to be. He had barely arrived when he needed to turn around and go back where he had come from.

In the coming weeks, their joy over their decision to get married was mingled with sadness over the death of the baby. Nevertheless, they were carried along by the excitement of their new life together. Just six weeks later, they were married in the chapel at the student center where they had met. It was a small wedding, with a few dozen family and friends. Sarah wore a long white cotton dress she'd sewn herself, and the couple gave out daisies to all the guests and introduced them to one another. The reception was a simple joyful affair as everyone danced and the two families got to know each other. Sarah and Juan-Lorenzo then left for an extended journey by land through Mexico, Central America, and then on to Bolivia.

Sarah and Juan-Lorenzo Start a Business

BY RAVEN

In December of 1971, Juan-Lorenzo and Sarah sat on a shaded bench near the university clock tower. In the first seven months of their marriage they had backpacked in Central and South America for two months, moved in together, finished out a semester at school, and Juan-Lorenzo had graduated with a B.A. in Psychology. That morning, he'd received a letter from the Danforth Fellowship Program. "Congratulations," it began, and continued to detail a dream deal: They offered a full ride plus stipend for a doctorate program that would end in a Ph.D. for Juan-Lorenzo as a clinical psychologist. The couple had made plans to celebrate that night, but Juan-Lorenzo sat looking down at the letter with a worried expression.

"Something doesn't feel right about this," he said.

Sarah turned to look at him. "What do you mean? What doesn't feel right?"

"I'm not sure I can explain it, Sarah" he said. "It would be years of more schooling, but I like that idea. I want to help people, of course." He laughed, "I even feel like I can see myself sitting in a nice office, practicing counselling, and supporting our family."

"I think you'd be very good at it," she said. "But…"

"I don't know. When I think about it, I don't feel excited. I feel flat."

That night, Juan-Lorenzo couldn't sleep and sat up by himself at the kitchen table. He realized that the thing missing in the practice of psychology as he knew it was a spiritual dimension. That's where the flatness came in. He found himself remembering the words he'd heard in his heart back in Hawaii. "I could do that. But…" That phrase had delivered him to the Catholic faith three years earlier, and he had trusted it then. The next morning, he talked it over with Sarah, and she encouraged him to listen to that "But…" It was a word that promised liberty, even as it imposed a limitation.

They knew their friends and relatives would think they were crazy to turn down such a good offer, so they kept quiet about it until he found another way forward. The problem was, the other way they discovered would make their decision look even more ludicrous.

Juan-Lorenzo had a standing offer from an acquaintance who ran a small import business that bought and sold inexpensive silver Mexican jewelry, the same kind, in fact, that Sarah's engagement ring was made of. They would have to explain that instead of following the clear and fairly comfortable path forward in the psychological profession, they had decided to live in a van while

Juan-Lorenzo worked as a traveling salesperson. A few days later, when he went to his advisor and explained his decision, the professor's eyebrows shot up.

"What does your wife think of that?" he said, skeptically.

But Sarah was already in motion, packing and donating their few possessions in their little apartment. She saw it as a big adventure. They bought a cargo van and together converted it into a camper. Juan-Lorenzo could see how the move would suit her well. As a bit of a tomboy, Sarah liked the idea of camping. As an anti-materialist, she embraced the imposed simplicity of a vagabond life. And though already a budding feminist, she nonetheless saw herself as the support team for Juan-Lorenzo's real career. Other than the desire to learn and become an educated woman, she had no particular goal in her studies, so she told him she was happy not to enroll for another semester. Juan-Lorenzo, on the other hand, felt determined but uneasy. Once again, he was choosing to let Holy Mystery guide him, and they would have to trust the journey without knowing the destination.

For a little under a year, Juan-Lorenzo and Sarah lived out of their converted panel van. They sold jewelry through the Southwest and California, parking at campgrounds or on the side of the road. Naturally, they got to know each other on a deeper level as the months went by. They prayed together and talked about spirituality often, energized by the recent transformation within the Catholic Church. The teachings of the Second Vatican Council were a radical shift towards the empowerment of the laity, and the young couple viewed themselves as closely aligned with the liberal tides of the 1960s. They found that they complimented each other in other ways as well. Juan-Lorenzo enjoyed casual socialization but kept only a few deep relationships. Sarah, who often felt socially awkward, shied away from bringing people in. Once a connection was made, however, she had a wonderful gift for deep acceptance and connection with individuals and with communities of people. They both felt inspired by the purity and goodness of spirit they saw in the other.

One day on their travels through New Mexico, Juan-Lorenzo had the opportunity to independently purchase some Native American jewelry and resell it for a nice profit. It was clear there was a huge demand for the beautiful craftsmanship coming from the reservations of the Navajo, the Zuni, and other Pueblo communities. So the couple started buying and selling jewelry themselves. When it became clear this was an income source with a lot of potential, they started to talk about settling down. They drifted north and west towards San Francisco. He wanted to introduce her to old friends, and they both hoped it would be a good place to look for a strong spiritual community in which to start a family. They also thought they might find support and make a go of a jewelry business within the *Subud* community. Bapak, the founder, had taught about the value of ethical business enterprise. He saw it as a way of bringing the mystical experiences of *latihan* into the world.

The Hinojosas settled in Marin County, just north of San Francisco. Sure enough, Juan-Lorenzo found two trustworthy business partners through *Subud*. His trade in Native American jewelry officially became *Dharma Mercantile*, and their business flourished fast. Within months, the need arose for them to relocate to New Mexico for a while. The business was going so well that they needed to be close to the Native American communities in order to buy and buy some more. Although Sarah was already pregnant again and five months along, they elected to make the move back to the

Southwest. They rented a little house on the north side of Albuquerque and anticipated their first baby together.

As a child of the 1960s, Juan-Lorenzo had a bias against business. The founding of a successful business was a deep learning experience. It highlighted for him his own prejudice and he learned how an organized business endeavor could be a profound experience of coming together for a common purpose, with a spirit of service and excellence. He discovered, much to his surprise, that he had an entrepreneurial gift. Providentially, the resources from the business also allowed him and Sarah to take their next steps into their future.

The Birth of Sabrina

BY JUAN-LORENZO

I stood by Sarah's hospital bed, holding her hand, and breathing with her. This labor was so different from her first. It was our baby, together, and our conjugal love and lifetime marital commitment had created a new space for me by her side.

A woman's labor is intensely interior work. It is a deep conversation happening in the depths of her body: silent at times, sometimes vocal. I tried to support her body where I could and do the breathwork with her, as we had practiced in Lamaze classes. The nurses told us the labor seemed to be going quickly, but I had already entered something of a state of altered perception. Time was measured through the pace of the birth process taking place within my Sarah, with

79

no regard to the speed of the turning of the Earth. The room was charged, humming with concentrated energy with her at its center and the rest of us upholding it with quiet intensity.

I moved to stand behind the bed and was supporting her weight, my arm around her shoulders, when the head of the baby crested and a new human being emerged into the breathing world. In no time our baby girl was in Sarah's arms, wrapped in a blanket. She had a full head of black hair, and her features were in perfect miniature — not temporarily discolored or distorted like many newborns. I gasped when I took in the sight of that face. She looked so exactly like me! Until that moment, being a father had been an abstraction. Now, here was this newborn infant who seemed to be made of the love Sarah and I shared. I lay my hand on her and felt the warmth of her tiny body. She was a little bundle of paradoxes. So fragile, and yet so incredibly resilient to have made that journey. So much a little animal, and yet so very much a spirit full of possibility already containing the blueprint of her own essential nature and story.

We named her Sabrina Clare.

In my heightened state, when I saw my face reflected in hers, I saw Holy Mystery in the flesh. I suddenly understood that life fulfills itself with every generation as it flows into the future. I saw that love is the first and strongest impulse in all of us, and its job is to transform everything in its path — starting with the parents of every child ever born. Seeing Sabrina's face was a visceral experience that propelled me into a state of altered consciousness.

In those days, it was routine for a new mother to stay at the hospital for a number of days — and so, of course, I stayed too. Although the shared room wasn't fancy, and the staff regularly took Sabrina into the nursery, Sarah and I were high on awe and wonderment. I became utterly present to both women in my life for those couple of days. The chatter of my ego that constantly measures my past and projects into my future fell completely silent. The processes of my mind ceased, and I fell into a state of unity with myself and with creation. In my first few days of fatherhood, every moment spent with my baby, flesh of my flesh, was a moment in the absolute *Now*.

Sarah and Juan-Lorenzo on the Camino

How does one summarize the decades that follow? It is quite impossible. Family and public life were a journey Juan-Lorenzo would not have imagined taking when he was young.

But the Inflection Point, that period of about a year he described in this book, led Juan-Lorenzo to Sarah and then to becoming the father of five children. Family life was a crucible for his growth and for finding Holy Mystery within the ordinary. His world of work unfolded from dealing drugs to founding a business into full time ministry as an ecclesial lay minister, educator, pastoral theologian, and founder of numerous programs and centers. Finally, he eventually established the "Solidarity Family": Solidarity Bridge, *Fundación Puente de Solidaridad*, Solidarity Medical Equipping, and the Solidarity Lay Association.

• • •

In 2014, at the beginning of Juan-Lorenzo's slow leap to what he calls "the last phase of his life," he and Sarah decided to walk the *Camino de Santiago de Compostela*. The Camino is an ancient pilgrimage route with paths all over Europe that converge at the Cathedral of Saint James in Santiago, Spain. The full length of the path they chose threads from Paris across the Pyrenees and has been in continuous use by Christians since the early Middle Ages. Before then it led to a Pagan sacred site. Knowing that for many centuries millions of souls had been paying heed to the presence of Holy Mystery along this same physical route, Juan-Lorenzo and Sarah both felt they would be traversing sacred space from beginning to end.

Thousands each year still walk the trail, sometimes for hundreds of miles, but Juan-Lorenzo and Sarah opted to go only the last leg of this path, walking 110 kilometers over ten days. Since they carried only daypacks and stayed in private rooms, Juan-Lorenzo called it "pilgrimage light" — a big contrast to the extreme physicality of his spiritual exercises forty-six years previous.

The path through Northern Spain was verdant and hilly, dotted with centuries-old churches, hostels, and inns devoted to pilgrims. The couple booked an itinerary that allowed them to leave early each morning and arrive in time to meet their luggage and have dinner at a picturesque, often stone-walled dwelling each evening. In the mornings they set out together, but then they walked separately for the remainder of the day. Sarah looked for a contemplative experience, meditating and journaling along the way. Juan-Lorenzo liked to meet other pilgrims, and he walked a little faster than Sarah. He felt warmed to the presence of Holy Mystery through his extensive research he had done on the history and rituals of the Camino.

It was an ancient tradition for pilgrims to identify themselves by a scallop shell fixed to their packs. For Juan-Lorenzo, those shells were also a signal that, on some level, they were all in this together. He liked to initiate a chat with some small talk about the hardships of walking and then ask the others about their intention for the pilgrimage. Each pilgrim seemed to have a particular challenge or life transition that had brought him or her to the pilgrimage. As pilgrims, they all were not just traveling, but seeking, and Juan-Lorenzo was in good company. His own intention was to be open to guidance regarding what he was calling his "semi-retirement" but was really more of a transition towards the next phase of his life and career.

• • •

Not long before the trip, Juan-Lorenzo had an especially vivid dream, one of only a few in his lifetime, all of them significant. He saw a group of mature brown bears, standing in a mountain stream. As salmon came up the river, the bears scooped them up in their giant paws. It was a simple scene, but he instantly felt it was a symbol that could direct his next steps. It meant that from here on out, his task was to work with elders. His vocation now would be to teach, share, and create with others who had also lived deeply their own professional lives in a way that reflected a spiritual journey. Moving away from full-time employment marked for Juan-Lorenzo a transition in focus, but by no means would it be a time of rest. He knew that he would make room for passion projects that were an extension of his life's work, which in a sense had been a passion project to begin with. The dream was a signpost on a road that would lead through parts unknown and ultimately to the final days of his life. For the ten days of pilgrimage, as he walked, chatted, ate, and slept, he had an antenna up for whatever Holy Mystery had in store for him in those years to come.

One drizzly day, Juan-Lorenzo was walking alone along a length of gentle hills. It was still early, and so far he had only met a few people, pilgrims going in the other direction. They had passed each other with the typical greeting of *"buen camino."* On the other side of a slope, an ancient stone church came into view. Pale lichen covered the walls, highlighting the dark wood of a heavily carved entrance. Leading out from it and down a hill were stone steps, worn smooth in the center by centuries of footfalls. Near the base the wall, the medieval masons had crafted benches for weary pilgrims to rest, with statuettes to contemplate as they did so. Juan-Lorenzo noticed a younger man leaning against his backpack on one of these seats, his walking stick still resting in his hand.

"Buen camino," they said to each other. When the traveler continued walking in the same direction as Juan-Lorenzo, they began to walk together. The man had a quiet face and darker skin, similar to his own, and was in his mid-forties. *Just a little older than my own oldest child,* Juan-Lorenzo mused to himself. The pilgrim introduced himself in Spanish as Paulo. Juan-Lorenzo could tell from the accent that he was a native speaker, and they soon established that Paulo was also South American, from Columbia.

After some small talk about the rain and the path, Juan-Lorenzo asked Paulo the question he asked every traveler that he fell into conversation with. "What brings you out on the Camino? Do you have an intention for your journey?"

Paulo had a ready reply. "I have a son in Columbia and, truth be told, he is lost. I had hoped to see him flourish at his age, a young man just leaving school. But he has no direction. And no foundation either. I worry for him. So yes, I walk the Camino for my son."

"Your son sounds a little like me at that age," laughed Juan-Lorenzo. "That was a long, long time ago."

Paulo smiled. "And you? What is your reason?"

"Well, I'm a Catholic. It's a prayer walk for me. I'm asking God for direction because my work life is changing soon. I'm moving into a different way of doing my work, as I'm getting older."

"Ah," said Paulo. "And has God given you any directions yet?"

"Not clear ones, no! I'm not sure I'll be getting any voices from heaven, but I'm listening in case I do. I believe the last time I felt the voice of God so clearly was when I started the work I am now transitioning away from. Fifteen years ago — so in the framework of my sixty-eight years, not too long."

"What a blessing!" Paulo exclaimed. "I'm curious about your work, Juan-Lorenzo, but first, how did it happen? How did you recognize God?"

Juan-Lorenzo could tell by Paulo's questions that he had some knowledge of the complexity of spiritual experience. He wasn't expecting a pat answer or understanding the story as a literal voice in the ear. Comforted that he was walking with a kindred soul, Juan-Lorenzo shared the memory of the last message that had deeply guided him in his lifelong conversation with Holy Mystery.

"It came in the form of a song, actually, Paulo. Well, I was already feeling like God was meeting and guiding me in this thing. I knew for years that I wanted to retire at 55 and be of some help to the poor in Bolivia. You see, I had been living in the United States since I was a young man. I raised all my children there, five kids. I

87

got my doctorate in theology many years before, and I'd already had a career as a theologian. Then when I was around forty, I had a forgotten memory pop into my head from when I was a boy in Bolivia. I'd gone with my father to the public hospital to visit some of his employees who'd been injured. I must have been very young, maybe seven or eight years old. But I was struck even then by how miserable and poor the hospital equipment was. I mean, I was only a boy; I believe I noticed the broken wheelchairs the most. Anyway, in my middle age, I knew it was time to give back to South America somehow and really focus my energies into what drew me to become a Christian in the first place: that the greatest treasure of following Christ is found by living in service with the least among us — with the very poor."

His walking companion seemed to take this last part in with some thought. "All right. And God spoke in a song?"

"Yes, it was another memory from my boyhood, now that I think about it. But not exactly. Let me explain. About sixteen years ago, I met a Bolivian-American anesthesiologist who had been very successful in bringing medical teams to Bolivia. We formed a plan to work together and to start an organization under the Catholic Church to expand that work. So, I went to speak with Cardinal Francis George, the Archbishop of the Archdiocese of Chicago. I knew and trusted Cardinal George from years and years back, early in my career. That history already felt like a synchronicity, a pathway laid out in advance by God. So I was walking away from that meeting where he had given his blessing to our plan, walking down the driveway, when I remembered this song. Or no, I didn't exactly remember it. It came to me through memory, but as from God. I remember feeling like I was walking on air. Do you understand?"

"Yes! Yes, I think I do," said Paulo.

"Here, I'll sing it for you." Juan-Lorenzo laughed in resigned embarrassment. "But my voice isn't very good!"

Paulo smiled and lowered his head to listen. Juan-Lorenzo began, sure of the song but, as always, a little off key.

Digo si, Señor
En tiempos malos, en tiempos buenos.
Digo si, Señor,
A todo lo que hablas.

The two men, one younger, one older, chatted some more before Paulo walked ahead and Juan-Lorenzo found himself walking through the drizzle on his own again. Always a list-maker, he mentally compiled the ways the rigors of the Camino were a metaphor for life, intending to jot it down before Sarah arrived at the inn that evening. One needed to pay heed to signs, walk in the steps of others, and go in stages; it was essential to be humble enough to make the journey in a way that respected your limitations (especially when you are in your late sixties). Despite his natural inclination to plan ahead, which he was well known for, Juan-Lorenzo reflected on a phrase he'd heard at the start of his pilgrimage: "the Camino will have its way."

• • •

That was the point. Traveling of any kind exposes us to a world of opportunity for missteps, and traveling as a pilgrim does so even more. As Juan-Lorenzo walked, he remembered his circumambulation of Maui as a very young man. He knew now that ascetic wandering is a part of every spiritual tradition. Traveling with a heart open to the synchronistic language of Holy Mystery seemed to have fulfilled some essential spiritual need in him. To be a pilgrim is to be a seeker, and that takes an act of surrender.

It had been just such an act of surrender that had triggered Juan-Lorenzo's Anointing Experience those many years ago in Hawaii. His spiritual life had begun like the ringing of a bell with the Mirror Experience and had guided him step by step towards the Christian faith tradition in which he and his family of origin had practiced. Because of the witness of Christ — despite the negative-witness given by the lives of many Christians and of so much of the institutional Church — embracing Catholicism had come to be synonymous for him with embracing love as a guiding principle. Dedicating himself to Christianity had required a moment of assent and surrender that would prove to be the most fruitful and pivotal decision of his life. There is an endless amount of work to do in a world full of suffering. To embrace a particular path as your own requires the humility to accept that there is only so much that is yours to do. Holy Mystery had reached out to show Juan-Lorenzo that his life was not about him; rather it showed him that he had a part in the work of transforming the world, but only if he so chose to accept it.

Juan-Lorenzo paused for a moment at the bottom of the last hill before the end of the day. The sky was heavy with what promised to be another rainy night, and he began to imagine in detail the meal that would be laid out for them that evening. Putting his hunger to one side, he walked forward up the path. He sang as he walked, this time, with no one listening but Holy Mystery and the hills of the Camino:

I say "Yes," my Lord,
in all the good times, through all the bad times.
I say "Yes," my Lord,
to every word you speak.

THE END

Appendices

BY JUAN-LORENZO

What follows are five theological/spiritual reflections on the content of this book. They contain concepts from many spiritual traditions, especially Christianity, gathered over decades of learning and prayer, that have helped me understand and live out my quest for transformation.

Next is a timeline of the major events documented in this book.

Essays

The Spiritual Life

In a real sense, everyone's life is spiritual. Spiritual consciousness and intentionality, however, are a matter of grace and choice. My own spiritual consciousness as an intentional dimension of who I am began with my Mirror Experience. From that moment, I became a seeker — someone who has definitively entered into a quest for a transformation of a spiritual nature. My quest was for a different foundation for my existence, one that would lead to a fuller, deeper, and more authentic purchase on life. My life before my Mirror Experience was based solely on ego-centered patterns and actions and was no longer tenable. I had been brought up short. I had lost my footing. I was no longer able to live as before.

Spiritual seeking has remained a dominant theme — a leitmotif — throughout my life. While the quest I have made throughout the period of my life described in this book did lead to a real transformation, the process never ends. My journey as a seeker is strongest and most palpable when I am centered, that is, when I have a sense of wholeness and of being grounded in the sacred. I believe that only the primordial longing produced by being on a spiritual journey can spur us forward in a way that is most teachable and guidable as our lives unfolds.

After my first mystical encounter in the Mirror Experience, I entered a period of intense spiritual discipline or asceticism. The result was that I learned to be moved by Holy Mystery just as wind fills a sail to move a boat. Notice that in this analogy the wind blows of its own accord. Only when the sail is adjusted will it harness that wind. Throughout this period of my life, I had to both create the sail and learn to use it. I was learning to use discernment as my guide.

•••

Coming of age in the 1960s, the concept of personal freedom was held up in the same way as those hippie watch words of "love" and "peace." But freedom is a complex thing. When pursued directly it leads away from that we most deeply desire. There is a great paradox in my life that relates to freedom. Before my Mirror Experience, I thought pursuing a life free from societal constraints and "hang ups" made me free. I discovered that I was not free at all and in fact the type of freedom I had pursued had led me to be utterly un-free. As I ultimately embraced a spiritual/religious path, I allowed myself to be constrained by the discipline of engaging life on its own terms — with all its ambiguities and apparent compromises and contradictions.

By drawing from the deep insights gained by spiritual seekers over the millennia who codified their hard-earned wisdom in culture, religion, and everyday standards of goodness (called "virtues"), I was finally freer than I had ever been before. Jesus' words finally came to life for me: "For whoever would save their life will lose it, but whoever loses their life for my sake will save it" (Matthew 16:25).

In my Doctoral studies at the Jesuit School of Theology in Berkeley, I recognized my Mirror Experience reflected and articulated in what in Ignatian spirituality is the concept of *discernment*. Ignatian spirituality, developed originally by Saint Ignatius Loyola, has played a strong part in my inner life. From my own silent retreats, to helping adapt the Spiritual Exercises for use by the laity, to now articulating how this wisdom can help guide the Solidarity Bridge Family, the mission efforts I have helped found in both the U.S. and in Bolivia, the story of my life has been and continues to be an expression of discernment, including the decision to create this book with my daughter Raven.

Most of us long for guidance in our lives. We look for advice in popular culture or from the people around us. We face the big questions of commitment and intimacy, of making a living, of finding a spiritual path, and of maintaining a fulfilling and sustainable lifestyle. If we attempt to answer these questions from an inflated or deflated ego (what many call the "false self"), we won't arrive at an answer that will lead us forward. There is a deep place from which human beings can draw to inform our decisions and choices. Some know it as a Higher Power, as Holy Mystery, as God. That reality is the source of all true discernment.

•••

This short essay is not meant to be an attempt to delineate the how or why or pitfalls of discernment. There are books and treatises on this. Yet some of the tools of discernment are quite accessible. For instance, in the Gospel of Matthew, Jesus says, "You will know the tree by its fruit." This saying directs us to look at the results of a situation to judge its real worth. We can ask ourselves: Is there more positivity in the world because of my choices and decisions? Have they made me a more authentic person? Questions like these can be asked of a single decision or of a more general life path. In the latter case, things may not be easily judged.

An extension of this discernment exercise is to imagine that you have died and someone is giving a truly honest eulogy at your funeral. What would the eulogist say? My guess is that real eulogists would explore how your decisions and choices led to a life that embodied truth, goodness, dedication, courage, and so forth. These all are fruits of a response, either conscious or unconscious, to what some have called "our better angels" and that I identify by the title "Holy Mystery. "

On the spiritual journey, through discernment we can rely on the divine reality to help us know when and where to turn. The traditional sources of any religious tradition, including scriptures and guidance from mystics, saints, and seers, also provide both a map and sustenance along the way. These guide us as we ask: What are my deepest longings and intentions on my own quest for transformation? How do my deepest longings and intentions shape and form me? Who have been and will be my companions on my quest? What disciplines will make my journey fruitful? And what is my ultimate intended destination?

During my intense ascetic period described in this book, I learned to be open to spiritual guidance in a way that would become a compass for the rest of my life. In that period, a recurring pattern emerged of Holy Mystery manifesting its guidance again and again. In response, I learned a posture of prayerful attentiveness that has informed every pivotal decision that created the story of my life up to now. Prayerful attentiveness led me to continue my education, to marry, and have a large family, to found a business, to pursue a Ph.D., and to create numerous education, training, and service efforts addressing a few of the deep needs in the world. In the final third of my life, this same Holy Mystery has again led me to found a number of related mission efforts that have healed, touched, and transformed many thousands of lives. In all these pivots and decisions, it was discernment that guided me like a compass along my unique spiritual path.

THE THREE-FOLD WAY

Recently, my family celebrated my son Mateo's wedding. He is the youngest of our five children, each one unique and precious. It was a glorious experience to be with my dear wife, all our children, their spouses, and our grandchildren. There are only a few sayings of Jesus that appear in all four Gospel narratives. This is one: "Those who desires to save their life will lose it, and those who lose their life for my sake will save it." I thought about this saying and used it during the ceremony as part of my blessing of Mateo and his wife, Mwende. To marry is to begin to live into these words. To have and raise a child is to live into them even more deeply, as parents learn they are not in control of their own lives. Marriage and having children can be the furnace of transformation that teaches us to meet life not on our terms, but from a source beyond us. Together with my work life and the many riches of the Catholic tradition, having a family has made up the central path of my own spiritual journey.

•••

There is a description of the spiritual journey that is very much in line with my own experience. It is the three-fold way of purgation, illumination, and union presented by many mystics and theologians, including Origen, St. John of the Cross, and St. Thomas Aquinas. This framework posits a spiritual process of three phases, or "ways," that build each on the other. Although they are presented as sequential, each way exists in all periods of a life, even while we inhabit one period more fully than the others as our life unfolds.

The *purgative* way is an intense process of letting go of the most egregious things in our lives that do not serve the spiritual journey. It is particularly marked by what in New Testament Greek is called *metanoia*, a change of direction in one's way of life resulting in spiritual transformation. We turn from what does not give life to what does, drawing not from the disordered ego-centered part of ourselves, but from the deeper foundation of the true self — that part of us that is in touch with and part of Holy Mystery. Because we are creatures of habit, this shift can be quite difficult and painful, and the false self may experience it as a form of death. This is how I experienced my own ascetic period in my early twenties. The illuminative way is a process of consolidation in which we receive nourishment and guidance from the wisdom of one or more spiritual traditions. I experienced this when the parables from Matthew came to life for me, then on my return to Bolivia to be reconciled with my family and new-found faith, and again in graduate school where I began to explore the deep well of spirituality bequeathed to us by those who went before. Finally, the unitive way is the phase when consolidation has reached its summit and we experiences a state of unity with the sacred, presumably as fully as is possible while still living here on Earth. Although I have had glimpses of the unitive way, I still reside in the way of illumination and continue to experience elements of the purgative way.

•••

In the intense spiritual period of my early twenties, the unitive way was most deeply expressed in the mystical moment I have called my Anointing Experience. It came at the moment I fully embraced a new direction, one that continues to this day. The direction I was led to take was not one I would have chosen before that very moment. However, my inner guidance was clear. It called me to be reconciled, to open myself to all the good that can be found in culture, religion, education, and in all that is. I was called to a reversal of the cynicism and judgmental harshness that had marked my life since military school. Like many young people in an educated, post-modern American society, I had an animus against Christianity and Catholicism. In some respects, the animus was and is well deserved. Yet without a spiritual posture of suspension of judgment and suspicion of my own habitual inclinations, I would never have discovered the spiritual riches available to me from that point on.

•••

After my Anointing Experience, I entered the illuminative way by beginning to attend Sunday and weekday Mass. I began reading and studying the Hebrew and Christian Scriptures and engaged in multiple acts of service. Slowly, ever so slowly, I began to feel the presence of Holy Mystery in Christianity as this finds expression in Roman Catholicism. I found it not only in the ritual life of the Church and in the Scriptures, but in my ordinary life as well.

The sources for illumination as a Catholic are rich and varied. Sacred spaces, Scripture, contemplation, and the ritual rhythms of the liturgy all play a role. As in most spiritual traditions, they include ritual, which conveys through symbol the truth at the heart of the tradition. You might have noticed in my story how important Scripture has been, beginning with the luminous parables in the Gospel of Matthew that spoke so directly to my soul. Early in my journey, I spent innumerable hours reading and finding encounter with Holy Mystery in sacred texts of many faiths. Today I continue to find nourishment in the form of meditation on the Bible in daily prayer. The rhythm of the liturgical year is another source of illumination.

Over the millennia, a liturgical calendar has emerged in many Christian denominations, which includes periods of intensity brought by the seasons of Advent/Christmas and Lent/Easter. The year culminates in the three high holy days called the Triduum: Holy Thursday, Good Friday, and the Easter Vigil. To allow oneself to prayerfully inhabit these periods and seasons is to be open to the symbolic universe presented there. The rites of the Church, especially the Eucharist, express the profound meaning of Christ's life, death, and resurrection. The Eucharist began with Jesus and his disciples observing a Passover meal, a celebration of the liberation of the Hebrews from Egypt and of God's connection with the

Jewish people. In the Christian celebration of the Mass that commemorates this ritual meal, we are told to eat and drink of Christ's own body and blood — a profound act of intermingling. This understanding feels primordial. To the modern mind it appears primitive, confounding, ridiculous, and even scandalous. When experienced with prayerful attentiveness, however, it ultimately holds a key to Christian wisdom. It conveys what Saint Athanasius expressed as "He became what we are that we might become what he is." Eucharist is a profound pathway to experience ourselves united with the holy, including the mystery of our communion with one another.

In addition to rituals, private prayer, and spiritual texts, as I walk in the illuminative way I have been nourished by Catholicism's traditional settings. Churches are great spaces for community, and monasteries are wonderful places focused on prayer, silence, and solitude. In fact, some of this book was written in Trappist Christian monasteries as well as a Buddhist one. In many religions, including Christianity, Buddhism, and Hinduism, monastic traditions are often held up as the best or only way to reach the unitive way. The furnace of transformation, we are told, is found in silence, ascetical practice, prayer, and meditation. While these are central to the spiritual life, I question this idealized view of monasticism. The transformative journey of career, marriage, parenthood, and social solidarity are the pillars of spiritual formation for the laity, and when they are paired with the resources of a faith tradition they can be an excellent path that leads to deep union with Holy Mystery.

•••

Learning to be a good father and husband has sometimes been a crucible in which I have experienced the *purgative* way and gained painful self-knowledge. Sarah has a way of letting me know, in no uncertain terms, when I fall into a pattern of blaming that is deeply ingrained in my character. It emerges when I am either stressed or when there are things that are unresolved in our marital relationship that need attention. Incidents where this pattern manifests cause me to take stock in myself in a way I have finally become familiar with. The fact is, I often lose the thread of my spiritual practice, and it takes being caught up short for me to come back to my senses. I need to reorient myself through the lodestone of the spiritual life — self-knowledge. Literally, a lodestone is a stone with magnetic properties, used in ancient times as a compass. Although a magnet is something that strongly attracts, self-knowledge in fact sometimes has the opposite effect. However, when we do the work to attain it, self-knowledge acts like the magnet in a compass, orienting us towards what we most need to learn in our spiritual practice.

The times I am reminded of my arrogance or blaming pattern illustrate that less-savory dimension of self-knowledge: the exposure of our faults. Naturally, we don't usually welcome this kind of knowledge. In fact, we do our best to keep it away with denial, obfuscation, and aggression. Oh, how we can resist authentically knowing ourselves! We are creatures capable of great wonder and giftedness, and at the same time we are so often petty and mean. We are sometimes magnanimous (large souled) and sometimes pusillanimous (small souled). The spiritual life is precisely about knowing how to cultivate our magnanimity and to manage our pusillanimity. Self-knowledge is a central dimension of how we are moved from one to the other. The truth, no matter how difficult, leads us forward into life and authenticity.

Self-knowledge is intimately tied to humility, which has been called the only possible foundation for the spiritual life. Although the concept of humility has lost its currency in our day, it contains profound levels of meaning that we neglect at our own peril. If we think we are in control of our lives or are at the center of the universe, we are lost. What did the word humility mean to the mystics? First and foremost, it meant that we must reach the threshold of knowing ourselves as contingent beings, that is, knowing we have been created by grace and draw our life from beyond ourselves. Or, to put it even more succinctly, humility means that we become teachable.

• • •

My Mirror Experience and my Anointing Experience were for me the first revelation of this reality. The knowledge of our own contingency is what allows us to become humble, and thus teachable. Saint Catherine of Siena spoke about self-knowledge as "the wood that fuels prayer." When she refers to prayer she is speaking about contemplation, rather than recited prayers like the *Our Father*. For Saint Catherine, contemplation was the act of connecting with Holy Mystery. I like to define it as the felt experience of the sacred: a disclosure that imparts knowledge that would not be available any other way. Religion, at its best, is a web of symbols that conveys deep meaning and speaks a word of truth to our souls. Contemplation is the experience of letting those symbols speak to us.

The many symbols of any spiritual tradition often have a single key symbol. One that unlocks the tapestry of the many. In Christianity, this is the person of Jesus, the Christ (the Anointed One), who lived in what is now Israel over 2000 years ago. Christians believe that if you want to know what it is to be fully human, you can contemplate this person's life and death. Christians also believe that if you want to begin to know who God is, you can find it expressed in this same man's life and death. For the Christian, and for me, the symbol of Christ's death and resurrection speaks of a God of unfathomable love and limitless embracing forgiveness. There is nothing I, or humanity, has done in the past, the present, or the future that can keep the God of Jesus of Nazareth from unconditionally and fully loving us. This means that I am lovable and forgiven, despite all the misery I have caused and continue to cause myself and others. It is only because of this understanding that I have the strength to seek out authentic self-knowledge.

VOCATION

My life story can best be understood through the lens of vocation. Although the term *vocation* has some contemporary currency, it has tended to be understood quite narrowly, either as a vocation to the religious, the monastic, or the priestly life or the pursuit of a profession such as medicine or law. In more common use, it has tended to be used for those going to a "vocational" school to become a plumber or electrician.

But the concept of the quest for and the reality of my vocation finds expression in many parts of my story. Vocation is something profoundly personal, sacred, and filled with weighty social implications. My favorite definition of vocation is that of Frederick Buechner: the "place where your deep gladness meets the world's deep need" (see *Wishful Thinking: A Seekers ABC*).

Vocation can be understood spiritually as something profoundly personal, because it engages us in our personal quest for the meaning of our life and for finding our place in the world. Vocation is about the creation of a self-in-the-world, something that is profoundly constitutive in the creation of identity. It is sacred because the quest for an authentic expression of vocation touches our deepest self, the place where our being touches Holy Mystery. This has implications because vocation is enacted and lived in the relationality of life in all its richness and complexity — family, occupation, community, citizenship, religious affiliation, etc.

I believe there are three dimensions to vocation. I think of them as if they were three legs of a small stool. Each has its place, and the stool will not stand without each being developed. and the stool will continue to wobble until all three legs each have reached their fullest expression.

...

The first dimension of vocation is literally *call* (*vocare* in Latin is "to call"). Martin Buber's famous quote speaks about this dimension of life: "Living means being addressed." There is a presupposition in this assertion that at the core of each life is Holy Mystery calling for response. The challenge is to believe that Spirit can speak to us and that we can become open to be spiritually guided. I believe human beings are hard-wired for vocation and it has something to do with both listening and responding. But there is much static that gets in the way of our listening and responding.

The call does not usually come from a clap of thunder or a burning bush. It emerges from our inner life and/or from our outer circumstances. For me, the inner dimension of call has always been strong. One could say that my Mirror Experience and subsequent spiritual experiences were a call, although their meaning was not obvious to me, at least at the time. The spiritual tradition of Christianity describes *call* as

an in-breaking of the sacred into our everyday consciousness in such a way that a dynamic of response is called for or
even required. I felt that sense of call in many instances, such
as meeting my wife, Sarah, and the founding of our various
work/ministry efforts. Outer circumstances also play a central role in call. I believe Holy Mystery is in circumstances.
"Reading" those circumstances to discover what we are being
called to do is not easy and requires spiritual discernment.
For example, the founding of Solidarity Bridge, the non-prof-
it/mission organization that exists now as of this writing
(www.solidaritybridge.org), came about as a convergence of
an inner call and the circumstances that make possible modern travel, Internet communication, U.S. affluence, and many
other factors. One could say that call comes in part from what
life wants to emerge, given the circumstances that exist at a
particular time for a particular person. Or, as my friend Bill
Droel of the National Center for the Laity puts it: "Vocation
comes at the intersection of an individual's talents and objec-
tive opportunity."

· · ·

The second leg of the vocational stool is *charism* or *giftedness*. Charism has as its basis our DNA, our personality, our
education (formal and informal), our socialization, and our
history. A question that tends to get at our charism is this:
What are your passions?

Charism is a biblical term that refers to a gift given by
the Holy Spirit *to* an individual but *for* the community. It is
connected with the same root word that comes to be translat-

ed as "grace." It is also about our unique entrée into the world and where our best contribution can develop and unfold and be fulfilled. From a Christian standpoint, charism is the giftedness of our natural endowment, enlivened by the grace of Holy Mystery to conform our lives to that of Christ and the way we embody that conformity in the world.

Charisms have often been associated with the extraordinary, such as prophecy, healing, etc. But there is a charismatic basis to all of life, and therefor to the ordinary Christian life as well. We begin to live our vocation authentically when we are able to tap what we have been given in our giftedness and use it for the common good. We each have an *endowment*. It comes to us from genes, family, society, culture, religion. When we respond authentically to God's call to contribute, to serve, to grow, we begin to access that endowment that is ultimately pure gift. Thus, I say that we humans are "hard-wired" to serve — God, others, life — with what we have been uniquely given.

How do you know you are using your giftedness? A sign could be that you are most yourself/alive in an activity or endeavor or when the state of "flow" accompanies your doing, at least some of the time. This has to do with the "deep gladness" aspect of Buechner's definition of vocation. For me, as I engaged life, I came to know my charism or giftedness as one that could be described as being a designer and builder of vehicles that help people to be in solidarity with one another and to grow and develop in their service to humanity. Another way my giftedness has manifested is in an ability to gather resources, both human and material, for my family's well-being as well as for the organizations I have founded.

...

The third and final leg of the stool is *mission*. It is out of call and charism that our life projects develop. Mission has to do with what has been put in front of us to do and to take on. This quote gets at the task of mission:

> The world would be poorer if every single one of us were not here to express God in his or her special way. In his autobiography, Romano Guardini tells us that in the first place God says something fundamental about each human being—pronounces a special set of words over him or her, as it were—that applies to that person and to no one else. Every human being is a word of God become flesh. And our task is to make this unique something God has said perceptible and effective in life, to make sure it is heard as the extraordinary pronouncement it is. — Anselm Gruen, *Building Self-Esteem: The Christian Dimension*

My mission has unfolded in the arenas of marriage and family and in the realms of education, ministry, and particularly in the founding of programs, centers, and organizations that in some measure enliven people and alleviate suffering and pain.

As I write these words, I am seventy-three years old. When I finished my tenure as the Executive Director of Solidarity Bridge, I felt an awkwardness to answering the question, "What are you going to do in retirement?" I frankly did not understand the question in light of my lifelong call, giftedness, and mission. I had given up my job and it's benefits and paycheck, yes, but my mission continued. Since that time, I have continued to expand what was begun with Solidarity Bridge twenty years ago and with *Puente de Solidaridad* fifteen years ago. We now have the Solidarity Family that includes these entities and other entities as well. There is the Solidarity Lay Association (sla-als.org) and Solidarity Medical Equipping, a business that has as its aim making accessible expensive surgical materials to those with lesser means. I founded these last two organizations after I "retired."

THE INSTITUTIONAL MATRIX

We live our lives in culture as mediated to us in and through institutions. These include family, schools, ways of doing things, and scales of valuing one thing over another. These institutions and ways of doing and valuing things impact us tremendously. Something I learned in military school is that we all play in a rigged game. This sense was further solidified during my anti-Vietnam War activity. What I mean is that we, in every structure in which we live — be they economic, religious, or political — create both liberating and oppressive structures which include certain beliefs and understandings that have been institutionalized to such an extent we don't even recognize them for what they are.

These structures bolster and advance some people and undermine others. Some of these structures are buttressed by distortions, lies, and power dynamics that many take for granted. As a young man, I naively rebelled against all structures. I was predisposed to not trust the "man" or the "establishment." What I could not see then is that those same structures can also facilitate and enhance life.

•••

The judgments that led to my distrust of the rigged game were on the whole accurate, as far as they went. They were, though, overgeneralized. There are aspects of our cultural legacy, be they institutions or mores, that have their own richness and deserve a central place in our societal life. For example, the Catholic Church to which I belong has a long history of betrayal of the vision and mission of Jesus. It is an institution that has shown itself as corrupted by power and the structures of sin that reside in a clerical culture to the point that it allowed for the sexual abuse of children and then its coverup. On the other hand, the institution is not all of the Church. The deep religious tradition that is Christianity at its best is carried in part by the institution but is also transmitted through the monastic life, the lay movements that are constantly springing up, and the liturgical life of that same Church. Thus, it is the complete Church, the "People of God" as the Second Vatican Council desribed it, that carries the entire symbolic/mythic deposit of the faith.

...

It has become clear to me that we must learn to discern where and how we can make a difference in the structures of all institutions of which we are part. We must enter into them deeply and, ideally, become well versed enough in their values and mission to make them better able to serve the people who are their members and the world in which they function.

Where we land in the institutional matrix makes a tremendous difference. I have been born to privilege, but also not. My Bolivian father struggled when he was studying in the U.S. to become a petroleum engineer. He was an outsider, as I have been myself in my many years of living in the U.S. But when we returned to Bolivia, I was the son of an "insider" who had a very prominent position in Bolivian society. I became the "insider" as well. When I returned to the U.S., I was once more an outsider, living in a poor Philadelphia neighborhood. When I was in military school, I was the "spic." And so on…. My life has been marked by experiences of both privilege and powerlessness. This has been a great grace in my life.

Yes, institutions are a rigged game, but it is the only game in town.

GRATITUDE

A quote from Paula D'Arcy moves me deeply and expresses in an incisive way how I have experienced grace throughout my life: "God comes to you disguised as your life." This insight expresses to me that all we need is already within the reality of our lives. But like many, I needed to break away in order to come to understand and experience this fact.

I believe gratitude is a fundamental dimension of a well-developed spiritual life. I am deeply grateful for the life that has unfolded since my birth until today. The fact that I was close to death a number of times from the heedlessness of my actions are a source of wonder to me. I am most grateful for all of the difficult things that transpired in my life, from the constant moving across continents, to my parent's divorce, and to the other vicissitudes of my life. They were constitutive of my movement into a vital, dynamic, and fruitful spiritual life.

More immediately, I am so very grateful for my dear wife, Sarah, the companion of my life for these last fifty years. She has been the bedrock on which our family is built. Her goodness and loving kindness have been so central to us having the five wonderful children we have, something I cannot imagine having happened without her.

A mark of a life well lived out of a spiritual vision is *gratitude* — not just for the pleasant "good" things of life, but for the trials and difficult "bad" things as well. May my overwhelming gratitude to Holy Mystery continue to imbue my life, especially as I traverse the diminishment that inevitably comes with age. May I have gratitude even for my inevitable death — the passage that will lead me to the fullness of union in the communion of love that is the Three-in-One.

Timeline

The Life of Juan-Lorenzo Hinojosa

Born – June 24, 1946, in Cochabamba, Bolivia

Moved to the U.S. – August 1946

Returned to Bolivia – July 1952

Parent's divorce – 1956

Returned to the U.S. – 1957

Military School – 1958-1960

Eighth grade and High School in Buenos Aires – 1960-1965

Oklahoma State University – 1965-66

Haight Ashbury – 1966-1968

Maui – 1968

Returned to Bolivia – 1969

Returned to Oklahoma State and then the University of
Texas at Austin – 1969

Married Sarah and graduated with a Bachelor of Arts degree
in psychology – 1971

Co-founded Dharma Mercantile – 1972

Sabrina is born – 1973

Christin is born – 1975

Dissolution of Dharma Mercantile and beginning graduate
studies at the Jesuit School of Theology and the
Graduate Theological Union in Berkeley – 1976

Monica Raven is born – 1978

Graduated with a Master of Divinity degree in theology – 1978

Damien is born – 1980

Graduated with a Ph.D. in Theology – 1981

Taught and created programs at the Oblate School of
Theology in San Antonio, Texas – 1981

Mateo is born – 1982

Founded the Central Texas Pastoral Center in the
Diocese of Austin, Texas, and taught at St. Edward's
University – 1987

Co-Founded the Central Texas Spiritual Direction Training
Program – 1989

Founded the Center for Spirituality and Work in Austin,
Texas – 1992

Began work for the Center for Development of Ministry at
the University of St. Mary of the Lake in Mundelein,
IL – 1994

Founded the Hillenbrand Institute at the University of St.
Mary of the Lake – 1998

Founded Solidarity Bridge – 1999

Founded *Fundación Puente de Solidaridad* and *Puente de
Solidaridad Internacional, SRL* in Bolivia – 2005

Founded Solidarity Lay Association/*Asociación Laica Solidaridad* – 2014

Founded Solidarity Medical Equipping, LLC/*Equipamiento Médico Solidaridad, SRL* – 2018

Wrote and published with Monica Raven Hinojosa *Full Circle: A Quest for Transformation* – 2020-2021

Acknowledgments

SPECIAL THANKS TO

My high school and lifetime friend,
Bobby Aguirre/Ram Sharan;
my wife, Sarah;
and my brother, Eduardo Hinojosa;
who were all interviewed extensively for this book.

•••

And of course, to Raven, without whom
this book would never have been born
and to Christin, for her beautiful aesthetic sense
in helping design the cover.

For Those Seeking Spiritual Transformation

AWAKEN THE STARS
Reflections on What We REALLY Teach
edited by Shannon Mayer and Jacquie Van Hoomissen

GRACE REVISITED
Epiphanies from a Trappist Monk
by James Stephen Behrens, OCSO

HOPE
One's Man's Journey
from Tormented Child to Social Worker
to Spiritual Director
by Marshall Jung

THE RETURN OF SUNSHINE
Poems by a Laureate for Ecstatic Grandparents
by Norbert Krapf

SHRINKING THE MONSTER
Healing the Wounds of Our Abuse
by Norbert Krapf

THE SOUL OF TEACHING
Encouragement for High School Teachers and Principals
Who Sometimes Might Need Some
by John Horan

THE UNPUBLISHED POET
On Not Giving Up on Your Dream
by Marjorie L. Skelly

Available from booksellers
or www.actapublications.com • 800-397-2282